A Bishop's Reflections

A Bishop's Reflections

Kenneth L. Carder

PROVIDENCE HOUSE PUBLISHERS
Franklin, Tennessee

Printed in the United States of America

00   99   98   97   96   5   4   3   2   1

ISBN: 1–881576–99–X

Cover by Bozeman Design

All proceeds accruing to the author from the sale of this book will go toward missional programs within the Tennessee and Memphis Conferences.

Published by
PROVIDENCE HOUSE PUBLISHERS
238 Seaboard Lane • Franklin, Tennessee 37067
800-321-5692

Contents

Part One
    The Church   7

Part Two
    Doctrine   49

Part Three
    Current Issues   63

Part Four
    Special Topics   95

Part One
The Church

Idolatrous Images of the Ideal Church • Many Raise the Critical Question • Measuring Success and Failure Is Difficult • Where Is the Church after Sundown? • Laity Are the Church • A Memorable and Hopeful Homecoming • Fighting In Church • Blaming Is No Solution • The Importance of Being Present • Dead Sect or Vital Church • The Necessity of Visions • Church in the World and World in the Church • Should We Market the Church? • Evangelism—More Than Membership Recruitment • Connectionalism As Mission • Loving the Church More Than Loving Christ • Size Isn't the Sign of Faithfulness • Ministry Has to Do with Being • Rationale for Itinerancy • Handling a Change of Appointments • Running Is Not the Answer • Idolatry and Popular Images of the Perfect Pastor • God Is Calling Women Pastors • When Churches Are Getting a New Pastor • When Pastors Change Churches • Stewardship and Access to the Table • Possessed by Possessions • Budgeting and Financial Campaigns • Dead Money and Vital Commitment • The Church Will Survive, But . . . • Name Sin and Announce Grace • Lessons from Korean Visit • Apportionments As Covenant and Mission • Wesley's Advice on Converting Heretics • On Compromising with Evil

Part One

The Church

IDOLATROUS IMAGES OF
THE IDEAL CHURCH

CHURCHES SOMETIMES HAVE IDOLATROUS images of the ideal pastor. The notion that a young, handsome male with a wife and children in the parsonage represents the best hope for leading a church is shaped more by society than by the gospel.

Pastors also have idolatrous images of the ideal church. Such idolatry prevents faithful ministry, distorts the nature and purpose of the church, and damages morale.

The popular image of the perfect church also reflects society's values more than the gospel's qualities—large membership and attendance, plenty of young adults with small children, spacious and opulent facilities in a growing suburban or urban neighborhood, high salary for the pastor, no conflicts, and every member totally committed to the church. Measuring success and determining morale on the basis of how closely a congregation fits such a profile is a demonic temptation of many contemporary pastors and laity.

A church shaped by the gospel has at least these characteristics: focuses on the worship of God, lives in response to the leadership and saviorhood of Christ, reaches out in agape love and justice to the world, has devotion to serious Bible study and theological reflection, treats all people as children of God; exists as a sign, foretaste, and instrument of the reign of God.

Of course, there are no perfect churches. Ideal churches need no pastors. Pastors are called and appointed to lead congregations in service to Christ. Churches do not exist to fulfill pastors' dreams of upward mobility and professional success. Congregations shaped by idols, whether those of the pastor or the laity, cease being the church.

It is easy for congregations and pastors to be seduced by the notion that each exists to serve the other. Congregations want pastors who will meet their unexamined needs, and pastors desire congregations which fulfill their unchallenged expectations.

Congregations and pastors exist to serve Christ. And, service to Christ is neither dependent upon the age, gender, or race of the pastor nor the size, location, or wealth of the congregation.

MANY RAISE THE CRITICAL QUESTION

A QUESTION OFTEN RAISED IS THIS: WHAT IS THE MOST serious crisis facing the United Methodist Church and what can be done about it?

My response has been this: We have an identity crisis. We don't know who we are as a church and we have lost our sense of mission. The church has become an institution in which even belief in God is optional or peripheral. Marketing techniques for a multiple option institution have replaced response to the gospel of Jesus Christ as the means of membership enlistment. The basic appeal is to self-defined needs rather than a call to radical discipleship. The church's mission, therefore, is to meet its members' perceived needs rather than to serve God's need for a redeemed, reconciled, and healed world.

The identity and mission of the church are rooted in God's grace and call. Recovery of our theological foundation, therefore, is essential. God, however, is conspicuously absent from contemporary church life. Serious grappling with God's presence, nature, and purpose is the exception in congregational gatherings, even when we "worship." Discipleship to Jesus Christ is seldom pursued with disciplined intention. And, participation in mission is relegated to a weekend work team or the passing of the collection plate.

Stanley Hauerwas has argued that discipleship is a craft. It has to be learned, and learning requires intentional and persistent practice. Discipleship means knowing who Jesus Christ is and following the revelation made known in his life, teaching, death, resurrection, and presence. The church's life and mission must be Christ-shaped and motivated.

In order to recover identity and mission, laity and clergy must refocus on theology (who God is, what God is doing, and what we are to be and do in response). Recovery of a Wesleyan emphasis on obedience as a necessary component of faith in Christ can save the church from narcissistic self-preoccupation and a consumerist approach to discipleship and mission.

Laity are raising the critical question. Let us all grapple with it.

MEASURING SUCCESS AND FAILURE IS DIFFICULT

REPORTS FROM LOCAL CHURCHES FLOW INTO DISTRICT and conference offices each January. Pastors, district superintendents, treasurers, membership secretaries, and bishops anxiously await the final tally on membership, attendance, budget and apportionment payments. Did we have a "good year?"

Statistics are important indicators and I hope that every church will grow in membership, attendance, and giving. Statistical decline demoralizes and may diminish the church's witness.

Statistics, however, are not the measures of the church's success. Membership and attendance increases are not, in themselves, signs of faithfulness. People can attend and join the church and even give to it without being committed to the church's nature and mission. In fact, we can so market the church with its multiple programs designed for everyone that belief in God becomes incidental.

Authentic success has to do with God's vision for the church and the world. How clearly does the church reveal the signs of God's reign? Does the church exhibit clearly the qualities God desires for the world? That is the real tool by which the church evaluates progress, and statistics do not always measure a congregation's faithfulness to God's dream.

God's vision includes a world in which all persons know their own worth and identity as redeemed children of God. Have persons experienced God's transforming love through our congregations?

God's reign involves the removal of racial and class barriers. Are our churches more racially and socio-economically inclusive than a year ago? Are they open to receiving and supporting members and pastors who are a different color?

God's reign includes "good news being preached to the poor." Is there less poverty in our communities as a result of the witness and service of our congregations? Are our churches champions of justice and mercy?

In God's kingdom, people are motivated by service instead of profits, personal or institutional aggrandizement, or power. Are our churches more service-oriented than prestige-conscious? Are our members more concerned about serving than being served?

In the final analysis, faithfulness to God's reign is the only success that matters. We thank God for signs of faithfulness and pray for the courage to live toward his vision.

WHERE IS THE CHURCH AFTER SUNDOWN?

I PARTICIPATED IN A RIDE-ALONG OPPORTUNITY WITH THE Nashville Police Department. From 10:30 P.M. until 3:30 A.M., I accompanied an officer on his patrol of the areas of Vanderbilt and Belmont Universities, Edgehill, West End Avenue, and Music Row.

Nothing dramatic occurred during the patrol. According to the officer, it was a relatively calm Thursday evening and Friday morning. Several things, however, did catch my attention.

I was impressed with the police officer. He was keenly observant and always professional. He handled a couple of potentially sensitive and volatile situations with calmness and kindness. He did a lot of social work and mediation and my appreciation increased for the complex role the police play.

The number of people on the streets and in the bars, and the crowds filling the sidewalks and alleys of the public housing units surprised me. A lot is happening while most church folks sleep. Midnight basketball may be a very good idea.

Another thing that caught my attention was the church buildings. They exist in almost every neighborhood. All were unoccupied and many were fenced in and bars covered the windows and doors. The contrast between the activities in the streets and bars and the inactivity in the churches made me ask: Is the church totally unaware of a segment of the population who desperately need the gospel? Do God's redemptive action and presence end at sundown?

A streetwise former drug addict and dealer commented recently that we church people seem to assume that the God issues surface in peoples lives only between the hours of 8:00 A.M. and 5:00 P.M. He contends that most people in the street are most open to God between midnight and dawn.

I'm not sure what all this means. Maybe one implication is that more than police officers are needed after midnight. We need to explore ways the church can make a difference after dark. One thing is certain: God's mercy and grace do not come to an end at sundown.

LAITY ARE THE CHURCH

WHAT IS THE ROLE OF THE LAITY IN THE CHURCH? THE question has been raised in one form or another in teaching/listening days I have had in the two conferences. Laity are vitally concerned about the church and their role in it.

First, laity do not belong to the church; they are the church. The church is more like an organism than an organization. We belong to organizations. As a member of an organization, we pay dues, attend, and participate in projects. We move in and out of the organization in accordance with preferences, abilities, and interests.

An organism, on the other hand, is something we are. It is our essence, our identity. We belong to an organism the way a bud belongs to a flower, a neutron belongs to an atom, an organ belongs to a body. We are an integral component of an organism and each component is related to and dependent on every other component.

The church, as an organism, is our identity. Our role is to live out that identity. We are the church wherever we are. Our primary function is to be Christ's presence in the world.

The principal arena for the laity's living out their church identity is the world—where we live, work, and play. The home, the factory, the school, the office, and the playground are the places laity fulfill their primary role. Being Christ's body is the primary calling for laity and clergy.

The church as an organization exists to facilitate, support, and celebrate the organism's mission in the world. We come together to remember whose we are, to celebrate the one who calls and empowers us, and to strategize for effective mission. Clergy and other staff have been set apart to assist the whole body in fulfilling its identity and role.

The role of the laity and clergy is to be the church.

A Memorable and Hopeful Homecoming

A FEW WEEKS AGO I ATTENDED "HOMECOMING" AT THE Fairhaven United Methodist Church near Gaithersburg, Maryland. It was my first time to attend that church since I served as the student pastor from 1962–1965. The church is the product of a merger between two white and one African-American congregations.

The homecoming has been on my mind during the recent discussions of America's racial divisions. Examples of racial bitterness, misunderstanding, violence, and separation abound. We know the divisions are real. Racism continues as a glaring and destructive sin in America. There are, however, signs and foretastes of what life could be like without racial animosity and division.

Fairhaven Church is multiracial with at least 50 percent of the membership being African-American. The chancel, children's, and handbell choirs all participated in the service. Each choir has about an equal number of African-American and white members. Even the "Gospel Choir" which sings traditional African-American music has white members. The pastor is African-American and the leadership of the church reflects the racial diversity of the congregation.

I remember when the contacts between the white and African-American churches began. The first group to integrate was the Boy Scouts. Then the women's groups (WSCS in those days) began meeting together and sharing common projects. The topic of the first joint WSCS meeting was "Race Relations and the Church." The Methodist men's clubs soon joined forces. Choir exchanges, joint youth meetings, and special worship services became logical next steps. As friendships formed and understandings deepened, being together in one church seemed an attainable goal.

Fairhaven Church is a reminder that hostility can be overcome and differences celebrated. Diverse people can love one another. One person who was a child when I was the pastor and whose parents left the church over the merger said to me, "This is the most wonderful church I have ever experienced. God's love is real here." People who were members during my tenure as pastor said things like this to me: "We've come a long way, haven't we?" "The dreams of those early years have come true; we really are one." A mother said, "I'm so thankful for this church. Here my kids are learning what Christian community means."

The world needs more churches that are signs and foretastes of what life could be like without racial animosity and division.

FIGHTING IN CHURCH

IT IS AMAZING HOW LITTLE IT TAKES TO GET A FIGHT STARTED in the church. Even the most insignificant issues sometime ignite controversy and result in anger, attack, withdrawal of financial support, boycotting of services, and moving to another church.

Conflict and controversy have been present in the church since it began. The two giants of the early church, Peter and Paul, were frequent antagonists. Paul wrote to the Galatians: "But when Cephas came to Antioch, I opposed him to his face. . . ." Most of Paul's letters are products of controversy. The disciples of Jesus argued among themselves and they seem to have continued to do so for two thousand years.

However, I detect a difference in the controversy within the early church and that encountered in today's local churches. Most fights described in the New Testament centered in theological, liturgical, and ethical issues. The meaning of Christ's divinity and humanity, the Lord's Supper, justification by faith or works, the role of Hebrew Scriptures, moral standards for church leaders, the relationship between the Christian faith and Judaism and Greek culture—these were among the causes of controversy in the apostolic church.

Honest theological differences and debate over ethical, liturgical and church polity matters have been occasions for creativity, revelation, and progress. Differences growing out of commitment to Christ and a desire to know and do God's will and being expressed with compassion and sensitivity are evidences of maturity and grace.

Much controversy which I encounter in local churches and the conference results from administrative decisions, personal preferences, power politics, and vested interests. The focus of the disagreements are usually property matters, budgets, personnel, schedules, program preferences, and denominational funds. Seldom are the conflicts theological, ethical, or liturgical in origin and nature.

The tragedy is not that conflict exists in the church. The regrettable thing is that we waste valuable time, energy, and emotional resources fighting over issues that matter little while the weightier theological, ethical, and faith issues receive minor attention.

Few things expose our spiritual immaturity and misplaced commitments as what we fight over and the way we handle conflict.

BLAMING IS NO SOLUTION

MUCH OF MY TIME AS A BISHOP IS OCCUPIED WITH responding to problems—problems with churches, pastors, conference committees, general church agencies. Countless hours are spent in consultations resulting from unanticipated and unwanted consequences—ineffective pastoral appointment, shortfall in funds, conflicts between congregations and pastors, inefficient bureaucracy, programs that fail to meet expectations, membership decreases, failure to respond to missional opportunities and responsibilities. The list is almost endless.

Roy Trueblood, in leading a laity retreat in the Tennessee Conference, gave me some helpful insight. He reminded us that placing blame and justifying negative results does three things: (1) leaves things as they are; (2) makes victims of those who blame and justify; and (3) disempowers those who respond by blaming and justifying. He contended that the United Methodist Church could be renewed if we would shift from blaming and justifying to assuming personal responsibility. It sounds almost too simple to be valid, but it's worth a try.

Mr. Trueblood encouraged us to assume that we are 100 percent responsible for negative results. We may not be responsible; but if we assume that we are, we will look for alternatives. Assuming responsibility empowers us. We may not be able to solve the whole problem, but we can do something.

What if each member assumed responsibility for problems existing in local churches and the denomination? We would cease adopting the stance of powerless victims and begin to contribute to solutions.

I remember a sermon preached by Harry Emerson Fosdick in which he stated that we are either part of the cause or part of the answer of every existing problem. That is a sobering thought.

Maybe it is time that we stopped blaming the liberals or conservatives, the pastors or the churches, the bishops or the bureaucracies. Perhaps we should all assume responsibility and join one another in being solutions rather than problems.

The Importance of Being Present

"NOW THOMAS, ONE OF THE TWELVE, CALLED THE TWIN, was not with them when Jesus came" (John 20:24 RSV). With that introductory statement, the writer of John's Gospel recounts the story of Thomas' struggle with his doubts about the resurrection of Jesus.

I wonder how Thomas would have reacted if he had been with his fellow disciples when the risen Christ first appeared to them? Of course, he was with them one week later, and his struggle of faith gave way to the affirmation of faith, "My Lord and my God."

If Thomas had been where he had been expected to be that first Easter morning, he likely would have been spared a week of terrible anguish. His absence from the fellowship of the disciples caused him to miss the presence of the risen Christ.

We have no idea where Thomas was when Jesus first appeared to the disciples. He may have had a legitimate reason for his absence. Maybe he wanted to be with his family during his grief. Perhaps he had gotten behind on his work and needed to catch up. He may have decided to just get away for the weekend. For whatever reason, he simply missed a great opportunity to experience the presence of the Risen One. That missed opportunity intensified and prolonged his faith crisis.

Let us not be too harsh with Thomas. We know what it is like to miss opportunities for deepened faith. How many times have we heard someone tell about an event we missed? We could only shake our head and say, "I wish I'd been there." As a pastor, I listened to many faith struggles around issues dealt with in sermons or studies and I thought to myself, "If only they had been in worship or Sunday School when that issue was addressed."

Sunday worship and Sunday School are weekly gatherings of the disciples. We gather in response to the Resurrection and in faith that the risen Christ is among us. May it not be said of us, "He/she was not with them when Jesus came."

DEAD SECT OR VITAL CHURCH

O N AUGUST 4, 1786, JOHN WESLEY WROTE, "I DO NOT FEAR that the Methodists should e'er cease to exist either in Europe or America. But I am afraid, lest they should only exist as a dead sect, having the form of religion without the power. And this undoubtedly will be the case, unless they hold fast both the doctrine, spirit, and discipline with which they first set out."

By the 1780s Methodism had become a thriving church in America. In England the Methodists were structured into class meetings, societies and conferences. The warm heart and the missional zeal had been institutionalized; and the survival of the institution seemed certain. Yet Wesley feared that the spirit and power of Methodism were already being threatened.

Wesley observed that the Methodists had become prosperous as a result of their discipline, frugality, and diligence. But according to Wesley, as they increased in wealth, the Methodists decreased in grace. Self-reliance replaced dependency upon God and one another. Complacency and personal comfort replaced compassion and identification with the poor. Self-discipline and accountability gave way to self-indulgence and excessive individualism.

Accompanying Mr. Wesley's warning of the demise of authentic Methodism was his formula for avoiding such a fate. First, the Methodists must hold fast to the doctrine of the faith. Knowing God with the heart and the head is one means of our avoiding having the form of religion without its power.

The second prescription from Mr. Wesley had to do with the use of material resources. He admonished the Methodists to avoid decreasing in grace as they increased in wealth by "earning all you can, saving all you can, and giving all you can." In other words, how we earn and use our resources as individuals and institutions determines our future vitality as God's people.

God isn't finished with the people called Methodists, whom Wesley said God had raised up "to reform the nations, beginning with the church, and to spread scriptural holiness throughout the lands." The world needs the Methodists to exist not as a dead sect but as a community shaped and empowered by God's grace.

THE NECESSITY OF VISIONS

WHERE THERE IS NO VISION, THE PEOPLE PERISH . . ."
(Prov. 29:18 KJV). Visions, dreams, and expectations are as necessary for sustaining life as food, water, and shelter. The absence of a pull toward the future results in retreat and death.

Nations are strongest when a collective image of the future unites the citizens in the pursuit of a dream. Churches are most vibrant when the members give themselves in commitment to a common vision of what ought to be.

When nations and institutions lose their vision, the people are left with only individualized and private hopes. Such individualized visions usually become narcissistic and competitive. Visions of universal justice and equality of opportunity give way to dreams of personal security and individual success. Biblical visions of a new heaven and a new earth are replaced with dreams of personal fulfillment and private piety.

God forbid that the nation and the church merely provide institutional support for our individualized and private visions. If they do, the likely result will be unbridled greed and pious egotism which masquerade as patriotism and faith.

Visioning is a popular and necessary process for congregations. The origin of the vision is crucial; otherwise, the church may pursue an idol. A church's future that is shaped by the collective desires of the members or the self-perceived needs of its prospective members will become an institutionalized version of selfishness and idolatry. Surveys and demographic studies, therefore, can be misleading.

The church is shaped by God's vision for humanity. God's image of the future has been made known in Jesus Christ. Discerning, claiming, and living toward God's vision is the church's mission.

The foundational data upon which a congregation forges its vision is the life, teaching, death, and resurrection of Jesus Christ. Bible study, prayer, and theological reflection precede surveys and demographic studies in the visioning process. God's will has seldom been discerned by merely surveying what people want.

The vision of a new heaven and a new earth where the hungry are fed, the naked are clothed, the sick are healed, the lonely and imprisoned are visited, and all people are treated as daughters and sons of God is a dream worth holding onto and pursuing. May God give us vision and the courage to pursue it!

CHURCH IN THE WORLD AND WORLD IN THE CHURCH

I HEARD A LAYPERSON SAY RECENTLY, "THERE IS TOO MUCH world in the church and too little church in the world." That is a thoughtful description of our situation.

Evidence abounds that the world's values shape the church. Studies indicate a wide disparity between church affiliation and the influence of the church on one's values and behavior. At least one church historian contends that the American church is the weakest it has ever been in terms of its ethical and moral influence. The church is so much like the world that historians of the future will be able to write the history of this era without reference to the church. There is "too much world in the church."

The church exists as a sign of God's presence and action characterized by love, justice, generosity, joy, and hope. There is too little church in the world. The world is in the midst of a moral muddle. The idols of individualism, consumerism, and hedonism have led us into an inferno of violence, greed, and isolation. Personal success, security, and happiness dominate our pursuits. Community has collapsed into isolation, mistrust, and loneliness. Compassion for the weak and vulnerable is pushed aside as naive. Personal integrity and unselfishness are sacrificed to the gods of expediency and self-gratification.

Robert Bellah said recently that "The church is . . . virtually the only effectively functioning institution in our civil society . . ." and that the world "may indeed look to it for a saving initiative." The church can best contribute to the world by shaping its life and work in accordance with God's saving initiative launched in creation and in Jesus Christ.

God is ever seeking to get more of the church into the world!

SHOULD WE MARKET THE CHURCH?

A MONG THE TOOLS AVAILABLE FOR CHURCH GROWTH IS
marketing. It consists of the church being customer-oriented.
Church programs, including worship and mission efforts, originate
from the perceived needs of people, and they are to be promoted in
ways that attract support and involvement. Demographic studies, sociological research, entrepreneurial leadership, and innovative
programming comprise the foundation for effective marketing.

The church rightfully uses solid demographic studies and sociological research as tools for understanding contemporary culture. The
gospel merits the best communication methods. Meeting the needs of
people is a central focus of the church's mission.

Marketing, however, is not a value-free nor theologically neutral tool.
The tools used do influence the message communicated. The medium can
become the message. One critic responded to the rationale that marketing, like a hammer, is a value-free tool by countering that people who
carry a hammer all the time inevitably begin to view everything as a nail.

Marketing carries with it the temptation to treat people as consumers. The customers and their self-defined needs easily replace God's
redemptive action in Jesus Christ as the church's central focus. Joining
the church is more like selecting a supermarket than entering into a
covenantal relationship. Loyalty is measured more by involvement in
the multiple options offered by the local church than by participation
in God's redemptive, reconciling action in the world.

Perhaps the greatest danger of building the church with the tools
of marketing is the distortion of the church's nature and mission.
Marketing strategies tend to create consumers rather than disciples.
When do persons recruited for church membership as consumers cease
being customers and become missioners? And, how do we offer multiple options for church shoppers without making discipleship and
mission optional?

The church's story needs to be told effectively. But, in the final
analysis, the gospel is a gift to be lived not a commodity to be sold. It
is incarnate in persons and communities who lose their lives in service
to the reign of God.

EVANGELISM—MORE THAN MEMBERSHIP RECRUITMENT

UNITED METHODIST MEMBERSHIP DECLINE RECEIVES considerable attention, as well it should. However, preoccupation with church membership can be idolatrous and may result in a distorted discipleship and a perverted evangelism.

The prevailing understanding of the church as a social institution which we join, rather than an organism into which we are grafted by God's grace, leads to misplaced emphases and truncated commitment. The emphasis shifts from discerning and living out God's vision for humanity to promoting and selling an institution. Evangelism is equated with membership recruitment, and discipleship is defined as institutional participation. Churches become religious shopping malls designed to attract consumers looking for spiritual bargains.

Evangelism is the sharing in word and deed of the good news of God's reconciling and transforming grace made known in Jesus Christ and lived out in the community of grace—the church. Evangelism involves living and sharing among the poor, the captives, the broken-hearted, the blind (Luke 4:18–20). It means being agents of forgiveness to the guilt-laden, couriers of reconciliation to the alienated, champions of justice to the oppressed, means of freedom to those who are captive, and beacons of hope to the despairing.

Discipleship is the unending process of being shaped and transformed by the living Christ and following Christ into the hurting, broken, and dangerous world God loves and for which Christ died.

Recruiting members and participating in church activities are important, but they are insufficient manifestations of evangelism and discipleship. Being the community of Christ who announces, through proclamation and action, the good news of God's reconciling and transforming grace—that is the essence of evangelism and discipleship.

Connectionalism As Mission

A DISTURBING DEVELOPMENT IN THE UNITED METHODIST Church is the erosion of appreciation for, participation in, and commitment to our connectional life. Among the evidences of the weakening of the connecting links are the following: the negative attitude toward and declining percentage payment of connectional funds; the prevalent notion that the local congregation is the primary or exclusive expression of God's presence and mission; resistance to accountability on the part of boards, agencies, local churches, and pastors; the drift toward a call system of deploying pastors.

Connectionalism is an integral part of methodism's self-understanding and mission. It is rooted in our theological and missional perspective and reflects our Wesleyan response to God's presence and mission in the world. Retreat from connectional commitment represents a fundamental shift in our doctrine of the church and our missional response to God's action in the world. The weakening of connectional participation can be a dangerous threat to the nature and mission of the church as traditionally understood and practiced by the people called Methodists.

Our connectional polity reflects our understanding that God's grace, power, and presence cannot be adequately expressed by any one congregation. The body of Christ is more inclusive and interdependent than any particular expression of it. It is the universal church that is Christ's body. God's goal is the transformation of the world. Fulfilling the divine good requires the celebration and utilization of diversity and interdependency. Inter-connectedness and mutual dependency then, are expressions of God's presence, purpose, and action.

A fragmented world made up of diverse peoples, nations, and communities, desperately needs the example and ministry of a church who celebrates and practices solidarity amid diversity, connectedness amid separateness. We need pastors and laity who know that the world is God's parish. We must avoid the idolatry of the parish being the totality of our world.

LOVING THE CHURCH MORE THAN LOVING CHRIST

I S IT POSSIBLE FOR US TO LOVE THE CHURCH MORE THAN WE love Christ? The following are no churches in particular and every church in general.

The local church is divided. Hostility and hatred permeate the atmosphere. Malicious rumors and vindictive threats poison the fellowship. All sides claim, "We love our church," and they genuinely feel that they are doing what is necessary to protect that which they love.

In another church, practically all the resources and energies of the people are devoted to maintaining the facilities and paying the staff. Although surrounded by people who need the gospel and the church's ministry, all the congregation's efforts are directed toward preserving and enhancing buildings and traditions. They, too, are motivated by "our love for our church."

Another church, which has abundant resources, strong programs, and extensive outreach, boasts of its power, prominence, and prestige. Its missional strategy has an air of triumphalism about it. People share their enthusiasm about their church with their co-workers and neighbors. They love their church.

A congregation is upset with their pastor because he has taken a stand on some controversial issues. He contends that the gospel shapes society as well as the individual. Members demand that he be moved in order "to save the church we love."

A Pastor-Parish Relations Committee protests the appointment of a woman as their pastor. Although she has the gifts and qualities needed to fulfill God's call, the committee contends that her appointment "will destroy the church we love."

Love for the church rightly includes a desire to preserve its buildings and traditions and a willingness to defend it against threats. Enthusiasm, boasting, and outreach are expressions of love; and concern for the tranquility and harmony within the fellowship is a normal goal.

However, when love for the church takes precedence over loyalty to Christ, the church itself becomes an idol. Defending, preserving, protecting, even praising the institutional church are not synonymous with love for Christ.

It is possible to deny the Christ in the name of defending and promoting the church. After all, those who crucified Jesus loved their religion, and even those who were his closest associates abandoned him while affirming their love for him.

SIZE ISN'T THE SIGN OF FAITHFULNESS

SOME CHURCH-GROWTH SPECIALISTS CONTEND THAT THE future of United Methodism lies in the megachurch, the large membership, multi-service, seven-day-a-week, something-for-everybody church. Small membership churches are seen as being antiquated, a sentimental reminder of a bygone era.

I have been privileged to serve as pastor of three large membership churches. They are great congregations! The varied and multiple ministries provided by them respond to the needs of many people. Their functional facilities, abundant human and financial resources, and strong leadership contribute greatly to the mission of the United Methodist Church.

The danger, however, is the assumption that size is the measure of faithfulness. Bigger, then, implies better. Some large congregations become triumphalistic and proud, assuming that their size is the sign of God's presence or the evidence of their own faithfulness.

Of course, small churches often succumb to the temptations to substitute cozy fellowship for missional involvement and maintaining the status quo for risky faith. And, despair and discouragement by small churches are as idolatrous as the triumphalism and pride sometimes seen in large churches.

I spend time in both large and small churches. I have concluded that when it comes to being a church, the size is irrelevant. Faithfulness to the gospel, forgiveness and genuine love among diverse people, a willingness to seek and welcome the alienated and broken, the presence of God's grace incarnate in people, authentic praise and exuberance in God's presence, a commitment to follow Jesus Christ into the messy places of the world—these are among the signs of a great church.

The future of United Methodism lies in congregations that live God's dream for the world—whatever their size.

MINISTRY HAS TO DO WITH BEING

A SURVEY BY AN AGENCY OF THE GENERAL COUNCIL ON Ministries attempted to identify the characteristics laypeople most admire in their pastor. United Methodists listed the following:

1. caring, cooperative, and honest
2. spiritual, broad-minded, and inspiring
3. self-controlled, loyal, intelligent, and supportive
4. competent, independent, determined, courageous, mature, fair-minded, straightforward, dependable, forward-looking, imaginative, and ambitious

What strikes me about the list is this: the emphasis is on being more than on doing. Members want pastors whose personhood reflects the gospel which they proclaim.

Carl Patton writes, "The making of a sermon is the making of a person." Preaching is more than preparing a manuscript; it is the growth of a person. Proclamation takes place as we live the gospel as surely as when we deliver a homily.

Pastoral ministry involves more than accomplishing tasks. It is a way of being in the world. Being present in caring, cooperation, honesty, openness, fairness, and faithfulness is ministry. A grace-filled presence which enables another to be touched by God's grace is authentic ministry.

I suspect that the qualities laity most admire in their pastors are the characteristics pastors most admire in laity. After all, they are human qualities which the church and the world desperately need.

One quality conspicuously absent from the list is passion for ministry, which emanates from a sense of being called, claimed and empowered by God. Jesus is the model for ministry, and his very being was the incarnation of God's presence, power, and purpose. Authentic ministry is always an incarnation, and such ministry is not limited to the ordained.

RATIONALE FOR ITINERANCY

THE TRADITIONAL METHOD OF DEPLOYING UNITED Methodist clergy is threatened. Some changes reflect the influence of cultural dynamics. Other changes are taking place because of the loss of the theological and missional motivation for the appointive, itinerant system. Alterations need to be made, but changes to the traditional Wesleyan system must be based on solid theological and missional grounds. Expediency, accommodation to the prevailing culture, or acquiescence to self-interest of upwardly mobile pastors and success-oriented congregations must not drive the changes.

The appointive, itinerant system is based upon three basic theological affirmations: Incarnation, Sent Ministry, and the Church as Mission Station.

God has become incarnate in Jesus Christ who embodied the nature, presence, and purposes of God. What God did supremely in Jesus, God seeks to do in each person. Every person has the potential to reflect the qualities of God. God has chosen the human personality as a primary means of expressing the divine presence in the world. Each person, then, has the potential of revealing God in a unique manifestation.

An itinerant system brings to congregations pastors with diverse personalities, leadership qualities, and theological perspectives. During a church's history, it will be shaped by the diverse gifts of a variety of pastors. Ideally, the diversity of pastors will provide a greater experience of the fullness of the God who is more than can be contained in one expression.

Congregations help shape the pastors appointed to them. Congregations are the body of Christ, incarnations of the living Christ. Throughout their ministries, pastors have the opportunity to experience multiple manifestations of God's presence and power through the body of Christ, the church. As no one person can contain the fullness of God, no one congregation can adequately express the living Christ. The diversities of congregations help to shape the pastors more completely in the image of Christ.

The idea of a sent ministry emerges from the apostolic witness as Jesus sent the apostles into the world. Throughout history the notion of the ordained being called by God through the church and sent into the world has been foundational. Itinerant clergy appointed by the bishop on behalf of the church is a visible sign of ministry as obedience to Christ who calls and sends disciples.

Since its beginning, Methodism has defined itself as mission. While other communions placed the emphasis upon the parish as a fixed community served by a parish priest or pastor, the Methodists defined the church as a mission station in service to the world. The pastor traveled wherever the need existed. The pastor was appointed according to the mission, not in response to increases in salary or professional advancement.

Changes made in the appointive itinerant system must incorporate these three affirmations: incarnation, sent ministry, and church as mission. Changes for the sake of professional advancement, personal convenience, and the self-defined success of the local church will sever us from our theological roots and missional vision.

HANDLING A CHANGE OF APPOINTMENTS

TRANSITION OF PASTORAL LEADERSHIP IS A CRITICAL TIME for both pastor and congregation. The success or failure of the incoming pastor's tenure partly depends on how the church and pastor are able to let go of the past and take hold of the new. Inevitably, a change in leadership and field of ministry creates uncertainty, grief, and expectations. Handled appropriately, the changes can promote spiritual growth; mishandled transition will damage both pastor and congregation.

Moving to a new congregation and receiving a new pastor involves a grief process. Grief is always accompanied by some guilt, anger, idealizing of that which has been lost, and attempts to recover the lost relationship. Pastors who carry anger or guilt into the new appointment almost inevitably take out their frustrations on the congregation. They put the new congregation down by idealizing the church they just left. Or, they displace their anger onto the unsuspecting members and cover real or imagined guilt from past inadequacies with grandiose plans imposed on an unwilling church.

Churches that fail to work through the grief over the loss of a beloved pastor make it difficult for a new pastor to perform ministry. Unresolved anger over the loss of the pastor often results in projecting hostility onto the new one. Refusing to let go of the old relationship manifests itself in unfair comparisons and perhaps continuing to look to the previous pastor for pastoral care. Or, anything suggested by the new pastor may be resisted as a disservice to the past.

Grief is a complicated process which takes time to work through, but more than time is necessary. Intentional efforts must be made to confront the loss honestly and constructively. Here are a few suggestions for both pastors and congregations.

Name and own your feelings. It is okay to feel hurt, anger, guilt, abandonment, and disappointment. Share the feelings with trusted family members and friends, but accept responsibility for them rather than putting them onto others.

Give thanks for the past relationships. Express gratitude for the previous pastor or the church from which you are moving. Gratitude is a marvelous antidote to anger and guilt.

Accept the unique gifts and opportunities in the new pastoral relationship. The best ministry is yet to be. God's grace is uniquely incarnated in each pastor and each congregation. Pastor and congregation may be shaped in rich new ways by the God who is forever creating new opportunities.

Invest yourself in the new relationship. Let go of old disappointments, mistakes, and failures. Forgiveness provides a new beginning. Permit the new pastor to be your pastor by inviting her or him to share your joys and sorrows. Pastors, accept the congregation where it is before trying to change it; give them the same acceptance which you hope to receive.

Accept the appointment as a gift from God. If the Cabinet made a mistake in the appointment, God's will is that you minimize the consequences of the mistake. Remember, the God who can bring resurrection out of crucifixion can bring new life out of a mistaken appointment.

RUNNING IS NOT THE ANSWER

D R. WILLIAM E. SANGSTER TELLS OF A PRACTICAL JOKE played on a college student. His fellow students put a recently killed skunk under the back seat of his car. Upon entering the car and smelling the odor, the student sped away. He drove seventy miles trying to distance himself from the smell. The student drove frantically attempting to escape what he was carrying with him.

Distance solves some problems. Flight is occasionally preferable to fighting. Separation may be the only means of handling insurmountable conflict. Getting away from it all often brings a new perspective. All of us need distance from our problems, even if it is only for a short time.

Most problems, however, are internal. We cannot drive or run far enough to get away from something we are carrying with us. Much flight only intensifies the problems and spreads the consequences to more people. The death and stench we carry inside rides with us to the next stopping place.

The decision to flee or stay requires discernment. It is not easy to decide if the problems are internal or external. But honestly facing our own problems is necessary; otherwise, we merely spread them around.

Pastors and churches face the dilemma regularly. Are the problems between pastor and people the result of internal problems of the pastor or the congregation? Is another pastor or church the solution? Or, will the pastor only take the same problems to another congregation and will the congregation only hurt another pastor?

After three years as a bishop, I am convinced that the appointive system often serves as a means of running from that which pastors and churches carry with them. It is understandable that a pastor assume that any problem he/she has can be resolved by moving to another church. Churches, likewise, assume that a change in pastors is the remedy for their ailments. The results are disastrous for pastors and congregations.

The Cabinet and bishop have the responsibility to determine whether moving a pastor is a form of escapism or a solution to problems. It is no easy assignment. We cannot do the job alone. Every Pastor-Parish Relations Committee and every pastor must be willing to honestly confront the difference between running from something they carry with them and moving to be in mission. The itinerant system was never intended to be a means of running from that which must be faced.

IDOLATRY AND POPULAR IMAGES OF THE PERFECT PASTOR

THERE IS AN AMAZING SIMILARITY IN THE PROFILES churches develop of the ideal pastor. Every church wants a committed, vital, personable pastor who can preach powerfully, visit regularly, manage effectively, and serve faithfully. Having an effective pastor is vitally important if churches are to be faithful to their mission. Churches know that.

Reviewing profiles and talking with Pastor-Parish Relations Committees have caused me concern about the popular image of effective pastors. Many profiles are shaped more by society's idols than the church's mission.

A widespread picture of the perfect pastor includes these characteristics: young and mature (ages 35–50), energetic, handsome, male, white, outgoing personality, family including small children who live in the parsonage, competent in everything. The popular profile presents several problems. For one thing, it says little about the pastor's understanding of and commitment to the gospel. Perhaps it is assumed that a pastor knows from study and experience the gospel and its implications, but it might be helpful if such an expectation were made explicit and the priority. Also, the popular image of the perfect pastor discounts the largest percentage of those whom God calls into ordained ministry. It means that women, ethnic minorities, and persons over age fifty to fifty-five are viewed as less effective.

Prejudice toward persons because of their race, gender, or age is sin. Rejection of one whom God has called into ordained ministry because of such prejudice is added sin. Acquiescence to society's idols of racism, sexism, and ageism denies the very nature and mission of the church. Furthermore, the popular image of the desired pastor displaces Christ with the pastor as the source of the church's life and mission. It is Christ who is to be followed and it is Christ who inspires and empowers the church.

Isaiah described God's servant this way: ". . . he had no form or majesty that we should look at him, nothing in his appearance that we should desire him" (Isa. 53:2). Perhaps even God's special servant does not fit the popular image of the desired pastor.

The most effective pastors are those who enable congregations to fulfill their mission as Christ's servants. Such effectiveness is not dependent upon gender, race, or age.

GOD IS CALLING WOMEN PASTORS

RESISTANCE TO WOMEN CLERGY BY LOCAL CHURCHES exceeds my anticipation. Having served for several years in multiple staff settings which included ordained women, I underestimated the obstacles women face in being accepted as pastors of local congregations. The failure to fully accept and celebrate the gifts and graces of women whom God is calling to ordained ministry diminishes the church and demoralizes many of God's servants.

God is undoubtedly calling women into ordained ministry. Resistance to them in the name of biblical authority or institutional survival smacks of idolatry and betrayal. It is, in my opinion, a modern expression of Jesus' lament over Jerusalem: "'Jerusalem, Jerusalem, the city that kills the prophets and stones those who are sent to it!'" (Luke 13:34). The *Book of Discipline* states:

> Appointments are to be made, with consideration of the gifts and evidence of God's grace of those appointed, to the needs, characteristics, and opportunities of congregations and institutions, and with faithfulness to the commitment to an open itineracy. Open itineracy means appointments are made without regard to race, ethnic origin, sex, color, marital status, or age. . . ." (PP 530, p. 288)

Every local church, regardless of size, must prepare to accept and celebrate the ministry of pastors whose race and/or gender is other than the one currently serving.

Beyond the sinfulness of rejecting persons whom God calls, resisting women as pastors robs the church of the blessings God brings through diverse pastors. Let us be open to all those whom God is calling and through whom God seeks to bless us.

WHEN CHURCHES ARE GETTING A NEW PASTOR

CONGREGATIONS WHO ARE ANTICIPATING A PASTORAL change confront particular challenges and needs. Appropriately meeting the challenges and addressing the needs can result in a strengthened church. Here are a few suggestions:

1. Celebrate the ministry of your present pastor; write a letter/note to him/her expressing your appreciation and support as he/she moves to a new opportunity for ministry.
2. Accept the grief inherent in the loss of a pastor and work through the feelings of anger, hurt, loss, and fear of the future. Avoid displacing the anger by placing it on the incoming pastor.
3. Talk to your pastor and Pastor-Parish Relations Committee if you have questions about the change. Only in very exceptional circumstances are changes made without the awareness and concurrence of the pastor.
4. Celebrate the diversity of gifts, experience, and graces of each pastor. Comparing pastors is unfair to everyone and fails to fully appreciate God's presence in others.
5. When your new pastor arrives, permit him/her to be your pastor. Requesting the return of a former pastor to perform pastoral duties such as weddings and funerals robs you and your present pastor of a unique opportunity and puts pastors and congregations in an awkward situation.

6. Pray daily for your incoming pastor and his/her family. Send them a note or welcome.
7. Attend worship the first Sunday of the new pastor's tenure and share in the scheduled welcoming activity.
8. Remember that just as strong pastors make strong churches, effective congregations tend to make effective pastors.
9. Beware of "gossip" about an incoming pastor. Real or perceived problems in a previous church do not necessarily mean problems in your church. At best you will have only fragments of the whole truth.
10. Be open to God's leadership in some new and exciting directions.

No perfect pastors, congregations, bishops or district superintendents exist. Therefore, every pastoral appointment falls short of the ideal. The good news is—God desires faithfulness more than perfection. May we all be faithful in response to the One whose grace makes all things new.

When Pastors Change Churches

WHEN PASTORS AND CHURCHES ARE ANTICIPATING changes in pastoral appointments it is difficult to over-estimate the importance of properly handling the transition, and both congregations and pastors must contribute positively to the process.

A major factor in a successful transition is the attitude of the present pastor. I offer some guidelines for pastors to consider. On the preceding pages, the focus was on the appropriate actions by the congregation.

I invite pastors to seriously consider the following:

1. Be honest about your own willingness to move. Avoid giving the impression that "the conference, bishop and Cabinet are making me move." Unnecessary and misplaced

anger results when pastors do not take ownership of their own desires.

2. Face and work through the grief process. Unresolved grief is fertile ground in which grow the seeds of rejection of the incoming pastor.

3. Use the transition period as a time for healing wounds and celebrating accomplishments. Avoid venting pent-up anger by "telling them off."

4. Make it clear that once you move you will no longer be available for such things as weddings, funerals, counseling, and visitations. Returning to a former parish for pastoral duties denies your successor the opportunity to build strong relationships, and I consider such action a breach of ministerial ethics.

5. Publicly affirm the gifts and graces of your successor.

6. Avoid second guessing the appointments of others. Analyzing, comparing, and passing judgment on colleagues' appointments is always done with insufficient information.The "kitchen cabinet" often creates a mess, and some people get burned.

7. Do not make contact with the church to which you have been projected without the awareness and permission of the district superintendent and present pastor.

8. Remember, all appointments are tentative until confirmed by the bishop at annual conference.

9. Leave your successor a list of persons with special needs for pastoral care.

10. Prepare for your successor the way you hope your predecessor is preparing for you.

Stewardship and Access to the Table

DR. DOUGLAS MEEKS, IN HIS EXCELLENT BOOK ENTITLED *God The Economist*, states that "Stewardship" as preached and practiced in most churches is based on the "theology" of Andrew

Carnegie, not on the Bible (p. 20). Carnegie believed that the Christian faith had to do with how surplus income was used, not how income was earned. The surplus should go, according to Carnegie's view, to the deserving poor, those who support the system.

Stewardship from a biblical perspective has to do with the management and distribution of all resources, including life itself. According to Dr. Meeks, God is the householder who is concerned that all people have access to the "table." He further comments that the biblical assumption is this: "If the righteousness of God is present, there is always enough to go around" (p. 12).

There is no shortage of resources for abundant living. The problem is access to the resources. Access, according to Carnegie, is determined by merit. Only those who earn or merit a place at the table can partake of the food. Those who haven't earned the right must come to the table begging, or eat the crumbs that fall from the table, or starve. Only those who have something to exchange have access to Carnegie's table.

Christian stewardship, on the other hand, is rooted in a Householder who desires that all feast at life's banquet. Access to the table is based upon a gracious invitation from God the Householder not on merit. All are invited guests and no one merits the invitation. God's grace, not human merit, shapes Christian stewardship.

The church is called to be a sign of God's economy. There, all are welcome around the table, and "when the righteousness of God is present, there is enough to go around."

Stewardship campaigns, then, have implications far beyond local church budgets. Stewardship has to do with who has access to God the Householder's table.

POSSESSED BY POSSESSIONS

JOHN RUSKIN TOLD THE STORY OF THE MAN WHO WAS transporting gold by ship. When the ship developed a leak and began to sink, the man strapped gold to his waist and tried to swim to shore. He quickly sank and drowned. Ruskin asked, "As he was sinking, had he the gold, or had the gold him?"

Luke tells a similar story. A young man with great riches approached Jesus with the question, "'. . . what must I do to inherit eternal life?'" Jesus answered, "'. . . Sell all that you own and distribute the money to the poor . . .'" (18:18–22). According to Luke, the man went away sorrowful, for he had great wealth (Luke 18:23). Had he the wealth or had the wealth him?

We might profitably ask ourselves the same question. Do we own our possessions or do our possessions own us? I know that possessions become addictive. Today's luxuries or nonessentials become tomorrow's necessities. I have become accustomed to a lifestyle that the earth cannot sustain for all people. I have been trying to reduce my dependency on things, and I have to confess that more things have me than I have things.

One reason Jesus warned against wealth is that possessions quickly and insidiously give us a false sense of freedom and security. Do possessions really increase our choices and options? Or, do they enslave us by creating an addiction to consuming and accumulating?

John Wesley considered affluence to be the most serious threat to face the "people called Methodists." He said that the only thing that could keep possessions from "sinking (us) into the hithermost hell" is to earn all you can, save all you can, and give all you can.

Wesley's advice was no cheerleading on behalf of aggressive pursuit of the American dream. His was a call to earn through honorable and just means, avoid extravagance, and share generously with the poor.

One test of whether we possess possessions or they possess us is how much we are willing to share with the poor.

Budgeting and Financial Campaigns

B UDGETING AND FINANCIAL CAMPAIGNS ARE AMONG THE most important, frustrating, and transforming activities of local churches and annual conferences. Adopting a budget and raising the funds necessary to meet it set the tone and course for the church's future. I have always found the whole process stressful and frustrating because of the ever-present gap between the existing needs and the available resources.

Budgeting and financial campaigns can be means of renewal, or they can demoralize the church and lead us to retreat from our identity and mission as the people of God. The result depends largely on how we approach the disparity between needs and available resources.

If, on the one hand, the shortage of funds is seen as caused by the budget being too high, cutting the budget becomes the focus. Retreat and reduction are seen as solutions. Little attention is drawn to the disparity between the biblical model of stewardship and the current giving of the people. Reducing the mission of the church to fit the giving of the people is a deceptive diversion from discipleship. The church thereby solves the financial problems by conforming to inadequate stewardship and laying the groundwork for further cuts next time.

If, on the other hand, it is determined that the shortfall results not from a budget that is too high but giving that is too low, the focus turns toward cultivating and motivating faithful stewardship. Facing our own failure to be faithful stewards is more personally threatening than projecting the problem onto budgets and ministries perceived to be too expensive. Confronting our own stewardship, however, can be a means by which God transforms us and the church of which we are a part.

Since we United Methodists give between two and three percent of our income to the church, it is clear where the real problem lies. The budget isn't too high; the giving is too low. Let us work together to solve the real problem.

DEAD MONEY AND VITAL COMMITMENT

I READ SOMEWHERE THAT BANKS IN THE U.S. HOLD MORE than $50,000,000 in more than two million accounts whose owners are never heard from. Those inactive accounts are referred to as "dead money."

Excavations in the Mediterranean area have turned up another kind of dead money. Bodies have been uncovered with treasures buried with them. At Pompeii, for example, corpses have been unearthed with the bony fingers still clutching gold and silver coins. It is money that has been dead since the lava of Mt. Vesuvius covered it!

What a shame, with all the needs in the world, that dead money exists! Just think what could be done with the $50,000,000 that lies unclaimed in this country's banks. Who knows how many people could be fed, clothed, educated, housed, and healed with the dead money lying around? The annual conference could start new churches, revitalize existing ones, and enhance and expand all kinds of ministries with even part of the unclaimed money.

Theologically speaking, there is another kind of dead money. It is money used selfishly while recognizing no claim upon it by God and humanity. Jesus told about a person who buried his money as a means of holding onto it, refusing to risk investing it in God's dream for the world.

St. Jerome in A.D. 400 referred in a letter to one who "preferred to store her money in the stomachs of the needy rather than to hide it in a purse." According to the Bible, the surest investments are in the kingdom of God, not in stocks and bonds. All other investments can be, and ultimately will be, lost. Jesus warned, "Lay not up for yourselves treasures on earth where moth and rust erode and thieves can steal, but lay up for yourselves treasures in heaven where nothing can destroy."

Money given to support the mission and ministry of the church is live money and an expression of vital faith. It is an investment in God's future which is secure.

Let us invest in the purposes of God. May we store our money in the stomachs of the hungry, the minds of the uneducated, the bodies of the sick, and the spirits of the oppressed and alienated.

THE CHURCH WILL SURVIVE, BUT . . .

ONE OF MY SEMINARY PROFESSORS SAID TO THE graduating class in the 1960s, "You will be the generation that experiences the renewal of the church or the ones that officiate at the church's funeral."

Thirty years later, the question of the church's survival continues to disturb church leaders, especially those of mainline denominations. Yet there is a difference between the motive behind the question in the 1960s and the 1990s.

When the seminary professor raised the issue with young pastors in 1965–1966, the context was racial violence, the war in Vietnam, turmoil on college campuses, the beginning of the sexual revolution, launching of the "war on poverty," the challenging of traditional institutions, and emerging of "the drug culture." The professor warned that if the pastors did not lead the church to be a reconciling and transforming agent in society, they would contribute to its death. The sign of renewal or death would be the church's effectiveness as a change agent amid racial hatred, individual and collective violence, personal and social immorality and injustice, and loss of community.

Today's discussion of the church's survival focuses on the decline of membership amid mistrust of denominational bureaucracy. Statistical measurements in terms of membership, attendance, budgets, and organizational participation are seen as signs of the church's sickness or health, death or renewal. Current prophets of the church's demise warn that if pastors do not lead in the development of effective programs to attract more people they will be delivering the church's eulogy.

As I understand the Bible, the future of the body of Christ is not in jeopardy. It has been raised and is alive forever. God's redemptive and reconciling grace in Jesus Christ has already triumphed over irrelevant religious institutionalism and personal and social evil. The Resurrection settled that!

Yet, the institutional form through which the body of Christ reconciles and transforms the world is always vulnerable to death. Otherwise, we would worship and serve the institution rather than the living Christ. However, organizations and structures are also vulnerable to renewal and resurrection.

May God use us as signs of resurrection and renewal.

NAME SIN AND ANNOUNCE GRACE

MARY HATCH IS A YOUNG THEOLOGIAN AND OUTSPOKEN churchwoman. She is quoted extensively in a book entitled *The Good Society* by Robert Bellah and other sociologists. She says that what is wrong with the mainline churches is that "they give out the worst schlock in the culture. The preaching and teaching people actually get in the church simply reify what people get from the newspapers and television. They tell people that what it means to be a good human being, a good Christian, is to fit in as best they can. . . ."

Hatch challenges the church to claim a mission separate from the hospital, or social club, or welfare agency. She declares: "To name sin and announce grace is the mission of the church." She contends that the church's greatest challenge in America is to enable middle-class folks to recognize "that their nice consumerist existence is killing them, plus killing the Third World."

The authors of *The Good Society* affirm that the church is in a strategic position to provide an alternative way of life to the competitive striving for more things, which fragments community, dulls the senses, and kills the soul. By naming sin and announcing grace, the church enables persons to persistently evaluate their values, relationships, and lifestyle in the context of God's purposes, forgiveness, reconciliation, and love.

Maintaining the balance between naming sin and announcing grace is the church's challenge. Some pastors and churches place the emphasis on naming sin, while others announce grace without naming sin. Naming sin without announcing grace leads to judgmentalism, cynicism, and despair. Announcing grace without naming sin, on the other hand, results in capitulation to sin and acquiescing to the status quo.

Someone has said that the task of the preacher is "to comfort the afflicted and afflict the comfortable." Of course, the tendency is to do the opposite. Comforting the comfortable brings rewards; afflicting the comfortable brings retribution. Afflicting the afflicted and comforting the comfortable are politically correct and expedient in today's world. Blaming the marginalized and vulnerable while rewarding the economically, intellectually, and politically elite is a popular practice in religion and politics.

Jesus is the church's model and guide. He courageously named the sin of the comfortable and compassionately announced grace to the guilty. He was crucified for "comforting the afflicted and afflicting the comfortable." In reality, he exposed the universal sin of humanity and the unending grace of God. Both the comfortable and the afflicted are guilty of sin and recipients of grace.

Faithfulness to Jesus requires that the church name sin and announce grace. Only those willing to confront their own sin can convincingly announce grace.

Lessons from Korean Visit

B ISHOPS AND PRESIDENTS OF METHODIST CHURCHES FROM thirty-four countries and six continents gathered in Seoul, Korea, in late August. It was the first time in the history of the Methodist movement that heads of the autonomous churches from across the world gathered as a body. The approximately one hundred and fifty leaders spent seven days in dialogue. I came away from the meeting with several impressions.

One, Methodism is a global movement with diverse cultural manifestations. The church is alive in Africa, Asia, Latin America, Europe, Australia, as well as in North America. Although the languages varied, there was a common understanding that, as Methodist Christians, we are part of a common family heritage and mission strategy.

Two, Methodist churches in many parts of the world are growing statistically, missionally, and spiritually. In parts of Africa and Asia the church is increasing very rapidly. The common thread running through the presentations from the areas where the church is growing is this: The church is theologically and missionally centered. In many countries, the church stands against the prevailing values and maintains a prophetic witness in face of real and potential persecution.

Three, in all countries, the church faces the challenge of maintaining the integrity of the gospel while giving it indigenous expression. There is inevitable tension between the kingdom of God and the world as it is. Being in the world but not of the world has always been a formidable challenge to the church. It is especially true today. Allowing for a variety of liturgical, musical, and behavioral expressions of the Christian gospel while avoiding being captured by the prevailing culture—that is a task confronting the church throughout the world.

Four, we in the United States have much to learn from our sisters and brothers in other parts of the world. I said in my presentation on the state of the church in North America that it is time for us to receive missionaries from Africa, Asia, and Latin America. We need the witness of our colleagues who have maintained a faithful witness in the midst of oppression and who are among the poor and dispossessed people of their nation.

Five, the Methodist churches must be prepared to enter into interfaith dialogue. In many places in the world, Christianity is a minority religion. Pluralism is here to stay! Learning to communicate with Muslims, Hindus, Buddhists, and atheists must be high on the priority of any faithful evangelist in the contemporary world.

Finally, we need one another! God's presence and mission are alive and well throughout the world in the church. God is not finished with "the people called Methodists." God's reason for raising up the Methodists remains valid: To reform the continents, beginning with the church, and spread scriptural holiness throughout the lands.

APPORTIONMENTS AS COVENANT AND MISSION

APPORTIONMENTS ARE OFTEN EQUATED WITH TAXES. Paying them feels more like meeting an imposed obligation than celebrating a covenant and sharing a mission. Complaining about apportionments and rationalizing default are more prevalent than rejoicing in shared covenant and fulfilled mission.

The newest congregation in the Tennessee Conference models an alternative attitude toward apportionments. The pastor and congregation requested the privilege of sharing in connectional ministries. Their voluntary gift helped the Murfreesboro District pay 100 percent of the amount requested by the conference. Such voluntary and joyful sharing enabled the Tennessee Conference to pay 90 percent for the first time in several year. The new congregation, which is still not a chartered church, already demonstrates the meaning of covenant and mission.

Apportionments are expressions of our covenant with God and one another. In a connectional church, each pastor and congregation serves as a link with God's presence and mission throughout the world. A break or weakness in the link thwarts mission and adds to the load of other links. Churches that fail to pay connectional askings leave aspects of our common ministry unfunded and rely on other churches to pick up the shortfall. Pastors whose salaries increase without payment of apportionments, in reality, receive a supplement from the church's connectional ministries, and they increase the load other pastors will have to carry.

Paying apportionments is a primary means of participating in God's global mission. It is popular to interpret apportionments as support of unneeded bureaucratic administration. Less than 10 percent of the apportionments goes to administration, and the administration makes possible the other ministries. No denomination has a more efficient, global network of mission than the United Methodist Church. Apportionments are the arteries through which life-giving nourishment flows to the hurting places of the world.

Viewing apportionments as a dreaded obligation robs pastors and churches of the joy of living in covenant and sharing in God's connectional mission to a hurting world. Paying apportionments is an affirmation of covenant and a participation in God's ministry to the world. May we pay them with joy and generosity.

WESLEY'S ADVICE ON CONVERTING HERETICS

CHRISTIANS ARE A MINORITY IN THE WORLD. EVEN IN America, where Christianity is the dominate religion, Christians live in an environment that is increasingly indifferent or even resistant to the claims of the Christian faith. Within the church, including

United Methodism, growing efforts are under way to identify and counter "heretics," those whose beliefs are considered contrary to accepted doctrinal norms.

Evangelization is a Christian imperative. Jesus commanded: "'Go therefore and make disciples of all nations . . .'"(Matt. 28:19). Witnessing to God's reconciling and transforming action in Jesus Christ is every Christian's responsibility. Preserving and passing on the core beliefs of the Christian faith are major components of the church's mission.

John Wesley was one of the most effective evangelists in the church's history. He proclaimed the gospel with fervor, passion, and commitment. He staunchly defended the faith, diligently taught it, and faithfully lived it. Wesley, however, devoted more effort to preaching the gospel to sinners than defending doctrines against heretics. Or, it might be more accurate to say that he defended the gospel against heresy by faithfully proclaiming it in word and deed to everyone.

Wesley's "Advice to the People Called Methodists" contains this warning:

> Condemn no man for not thinking as you think: let everyone enjoy the full and free liberty of thinking for himself; let every man use his own judgment, since every man must give an account of himself to God. Abhor every approach, in any kind of degree, to the spirit of persecution. If you cannot reason or persuade a man into the truth, never attempt to force him into it. If love will not compel him to come in, leave him to God, the Judge of all.

Since the heart of Christianity is love for God and neighbor, coercion and persecution in the name of witnessing or defending the Christian faith betrays the gospel.

The component most lacking among the heirs of John Wesley is love, not doctrinal clarity or intellectual understanding. Without love for those for whom Christ died, especially the outcasts and sinners, all efforts to defend doctrines against heretics only create more of them. God has chosen incarnate love as the means of reconciling and transforming the world. The church can do no less.

On Compromising with Evil

T HE WEAKNESS OF THE CONTEMPORARY CHURCH'S MORAL influence has a long history. The erosion of the church's moral authority can be traced to its willingness to compromise the gospel in order to win popular support. The irony is that often the motive for the compromise has been evangelism.

John Wesley contended that the church began to lose its influence when the Roman Emperor Constantine bestowed special favors upon the Christian Church and its clergy. In order to maintain the support of the emperor and the population, the church tailored the message so as not to risk rejection by the powerful, influential, and wealthy. According to Wesley, the clergy became "chaplains" of the prevailing culture in order to preserve their privileged position.

Toward the end of his life, Wesley traveled across England to survey the work of the Methodists. Although the movement had grown from a membership of four in 1729 to seventy thousand in 1787, he saw signs that Methodism was becoming a "dead sect." Instead of bringing forth "grapes," it was bringing forth "wild grapes." (See his sermon "On God's Vineyard.") For Wesley, the growing affluence of the Methodists was leading them away from the gospel and the poor. They were becoming preoccupied with preserving their own privilege.

The organizing conference of the Methodist Church in America (1784) adopted a strong anti-slavery position. No Methodist could own slaves or participate in the slave trade. It labeled slavery as a vile evil. However, the anti-slavery position proved to be unpopular among many Methodists. Therefore, the next general conference compromised the position in the name of church growth. By 1808, the general conference, for all practical purposes, nullified its opposition to slavery and even printed a special copy of the *Discipline* for South Carolina "in which the section and rule on slavery be left out."

A growing number of historians are documenting the church's acquiescence to evil in the name of increasing the church's membership. The Methodists, including Asbury, began to soften or silence their denunciation of slavery in the name of "saving souls." I contend that many of the doctrinal and theological conflicts in the church today have their roots in the theological contortions performed two hundred years ago in the attempt to justify slavery and sixteen hundred years ago in the attempt to preserve special privileged position in the Western culture.

We have reason to be deeply concerned about the membership strength of the United Methodist Church. However, of even greater concern is the moral strength of the church. God deliver us from acquiescing to evil and calling it "evangelism."

Part Two
Doctrine

Salvation by Faith—One of the Essentials • A Needed Word from John Wesley • Faith Includes Reluctant Obedience • Wesley's Aldersgate Experience • United Methodists Are Not Indifferent to Doctrine • Will Methodism Be Renewed Again? • Strong Beliefs and Tolerance Belong Together • Sin Is Real • Christ's Commands Are Covered • The Apostles' Creed Is a Pledge of Allegiance

Part Two
Doctrine

SALVATION BY FAITH— ONE OF THE ESSENTIALS

J OHN WESLEY BELIEVED THAT WHEN IT comes to beliefs "which do not strike at the root of Christianity, we think and let think." Freedom of thought has been a hallmark of Methodism, and the United Methodist Church is broad enough in its theological perspectives to include a variety of opinions. As one who has not always been a United Methodist, I greatly appreciate the freedom to struggle with the questions that defy uniform answers.

Freedom to think and let think, however, does not imply indifference nor a relativism which has no root. Unfortunately, some people assume that one "can believe anything and be a Methodist." One reason that we are so susceptible to needless controversies and popular heresies is our lack of familiarity with basic United Methodist doctrine.

June 11, 1738, two weeks after his "heartwarming experience" at Aldersgate, John Wesley preached a sermon at St. Mary's Church, Oxford. The sermon was entitled "Salvation by Faith" and the text was Ephesians 2:8, "For by grace you have been saved through faith. . . ." It was one of Wesley's favorite texts having preached on it some 133 times.

In his sermon before the learned people of Oxford, Wesley affirmed that "salvation by faith strikes at the root" of Christianity. He proclaimed that salvation by faith is the only hope for reforming sinful humanity and society.

Have we lost salvation by faith as a central doctrine and reality of teaching and preaching? It can be proclaimed so glibly and with little connection to life, and it can be reduced to mere pious language or cozy religious feelings. Yet, for Wesley and Saint Paul, salvation by faith radically transforms people. Nothing remains the same once God's saving grace in Jesus Christ becomes central.

Popular means to salvation seldom include faith, even within the church. We assume that our problems can be solved and wholeness achieved by our own cleverness or possessions or power or connections. We have been so captured by the exchange logic of the market economy that we assume we can exchange something for our salvation. The notion that God has taken the initiative and offers freedom from all that enslaves and destroys humanity runs counter to our desire to control and merit our destiny.

I wonder what changes would take place in our lives and in our congregations if salvation by faith became central in our preaching, teaching, and mission? Struggling to clarify the meaning of this core doctrine for our time should receive priority attention by all of us.

A NEEDED WORD FROM JOHN WESLEY

JOHN WESLEY SPENT HIS LIFE INTERPRETING, DEFENDING, proclaiming, and living the basic tenets of the Christian faith. He faced formidable opposition from some within the established church and many unrelated to the church. He was charged as being an "enthusiast" or fanatic, and he often engaged in debate over beliefs.

Wesley, however, maintained that in Christ we are all one. His words, in a sermon entitled "The Lord Our Righteousness," serve as an appropriate caution in the midst of controversies within the church.

> How dreadful and how innumerable are the contests which have arisen about religion! And not only among the children of this world, among those who knew not what true religion was; but even among the children of God, those who had experienced "the Kingdom of God within them. . . . "How many of these in all ages, instead of joining together against the common enemy, have turned their weapons against each other, and so not only wasted their precious time but hurt one another's spirits, weakened each other's hands, and so hindered the great work of their common Master! How many of the weak have hereby been offended! How many of the "lame turned out of the way!" How many sinners confirmed in their disregard of all religion and their contempt of those that profess it.

As we grapple with the diversity of beliefs and perspectives within the church, let us remain faithful to our Wesleyan heritage which declares: "In essentials, unity; in nonessentials liberty; and in all things, charity."

FAITH INCLUDES RELUCTANT OBEDIENCE

TWO PIVOTAL EVENTS OF JOHN WESLEY'S SPIRITUAL journey occurred during the eleven months between May 24, 1728, and April 2, 1739. Wesley described the event that took place on May 24, 1738, this way:

> In the evening I went very unwillingly to a society in Aldersgate Street, where one was reading Luther's preface to the Epistle to the Romans. About a quarter before nine, while he was describing the change which God works in the heart through faith in Christ, I felt my heart strangely warmed. I felt I did trust in Christ, Christ alone for salvation. And as assurance was given me, that he had taken away my sins, even mine, and saved me from the law of sin and death.

At the urging of George Whitefield and after intense, prayerful struggle, Wesley went to Bristol in late March 1739 to engage in "preaching in the fields." He wrote in his journal:

> I could scarce reconcile myself at first to this strange way of preaching in the fields, of which he [Whitefield] set me an example on Sunday; having been all my life . . . so tenacious of every point relating to decency and order, that I should have thought the saving of souls almost a sin, if it had not been done in church.

On April 2 Wesley preached out of doors for the first time, taking as his text, "The Spirit of the Lord is upon me, because he hath anointed me to preach the Gospel to the poor. . . . " Approximately three thousand people, mostly the poor and disenfranchised, heard Wesley's first outdoor sermon.

It is important to note that Wesley entered the Aldersgate and Bristol events reluctantly. The notion that we are "to do good only when our hearts are inclined to do so" Wesley considered a "devilish doctrine." Faith is obedience whether or not we feel inclined to obey. Had Wesley done only that which felt good, the Methodists would not exist. And, if Wesley had confined his religion to a heartwarming experience and not translated the inner assurance into outward witness among the poor, England's history and ours would be radically different.

Pivotal events often result from reluctant obedience. Discipleship and faith mature as we respond to Jesus' call "Come, follow me."

WESLEY'S ALDERSGATE EXPERIENCE

UNITED METHODISTS RIGHTLY MAKE MUCH OF JOHN Wesley's experience at Aldersgate Street, May 24, 1738. Wesley's experience at Aldersgate Street, though pivotal, did not occur in a vacuum. Preceding and following his personal assurance of forgiveness and freedom on May 24, 1738, were years of spiritual struggle. Indeed, Wesley's heartwarming experience cannot be separated from the disciplined pursuit of holiness which began as a child in the Epworth Rectory and continued all his life. Nor can it be divorced from his failure as a missionary in Georgia, from which he returned to England in January 1738.

Wesley was concerned with the "order of salvation." He states in his journal that prior to May 24, 1738, he sought holiness through outward obedience and works of the law. In his "order of salvation" one was to be "sanctified" and then "justified" before God. The assurance of forgiveness and freedom which came in a fresh way at Aldersgate reversed the order. Because he was forgiven, justified, he now sought holiness of heart and life in response to grace.

Doubts and struggles continued throughout Wesley's life. However, the doubts and struggles took place in the context of an assurance of grace and forgiveness. Personal spiritual disciplines and works of justice and mercy continued throughout his long life and ministry.

As heirs of Wesley, we continue a spiritual journey that requires personal discipline and obedience as well as works of compassion and justice. The journey is in response to God's prevenient, justifying, and sanctifying grace which comes to us in multiple experiences.

UNITED METHODISTS ARE NOT INDIFFERENT TO DOCTRINE

A WIDESPREAD MISPERCEPTION IS THAT UNITED METHODISTS do not take doctrines and beliefs seriously. Although we do not have one prescribed creed, we strongly affirm such core Christian doctrines as these: the trinity—Father, Son and Holy Spirit; salvation in and through Jesus Christ; the activity of the Holy Spirit both in personal experience and in the community of believers; the universal church, the reign of God as both a present and future reality; the authority of Scripture in matters of faith; and the essential oneness of the church in Jesus Christ. These are beliefs which we share with other communions.

Within the core of historic Christian beliefs, United Methodists have traditionally proclaimed the following emphases:

- the fullness of God's grace—prevenient, justifying, and sanctifying
- the essential unity of faith and works

- salvation as personal and social
- the church as a nurturing and missional community
- knowledge and vital piety as inseparable components of faith
- holiness of heart and life or Christian perfection as gifts and works of God's grace
- connectionalism as an expression of the church's oneness and mission
- the inextricable link between Christian doctrine and Christian living

John Wesley declared that God had raised up "the people called Methodists" in order "to reform the nation, beginning with the church, and to spread scriptural holiness throughout the lands." Fulfilling that mission requires that we reclaim our foundational doctrines and historic emphases.

WILL METHODISM BE RENEWED AGAIN?

IN "THOUGHTS UPON METHODISM," WRITTEN IN 1786, JOHN Wesley expressed the fear that the Methodists would exist only as "a dead sect, having the form of religion without the power." He added: "This undoubtedly will be the case, unless they hold fast both the doctrine, spirit, and discipline with which they first set out."

Wesley proceeded to admonish the Methodists to remain steadfast in the fundamental doctrine of salvation wrought by God's grace and expressed in righteousness and holiness. He then states that Methodism seemed to die away but it was revived in 1738.

Mr. Wesley attributed the revival of Methodism in 1738 to preaching in the fields. He consciously turned toward the poor and spent his long life among them, preaching, teaching, providing medical care, education, food, and shelter. He loved the poor and they became a means of grace to Wesley as surely as he was a means of grace to them.

The most serious threat to the Methodists of eighteenth-century England, according to Wesley, was their growing wealth and affluence. The Methodists were becoming prosperous and were losing their dependence on grace and their relationship with the poor. Wesley was convinced that if the Methodists lost their roots among the poor, they would exist as "a dead sect, having the form of religion without the power."

The United Methodist Church in America is predominantly middle class. Unless we rediscover our roots among the rural and urban poor, the United Methodist Church will lose its soul.

God is calling us to a conscious, intentional turning toward the poor as recipients and channels of God's grace. Nothing short of an institutional transformation is required, for as a denomination we have become enslaved by middle-class values, management processes, curriculum resources, and programmatic emphases.

May we, as an annual conference and local churches, turn toward those about whom the Christ said, "Inasmuch as you have done to one of the least of these you have done unto me."

STRONG BELIEFS AND TOLERANCE BELONG TOGETHER

THE PRINCIPLE THAT RUNS THROUGH WESLEY'S LIFE AND work is this: "In essentials, unity; in nonessentials, freedom; in all things, charity." In "The Character of a Methodist" (1742), Wesley wrote, "as to all opinions that do not strike at the root of Christianity, we think and let think."

Wesley preached and defended the historic doctrines of the church. He countered heresy and hypocrisy wherever he found them. He was not hesitant to disagree with those who struck at "the root of Christianity." He held strong convictions and opinions and he was not timid in sharing them.

Wesley, however, felt no compulsion to require that others conform to his ideas. He combined strong adherence to historic doctrine with a responsible tolerance of other people's convictions. He avoided the trap of both intolerant dogmatism and apathetic tolerance.

How difficult it is to have both a strong commitment to "the root of Christianity" and a tolerance of those who strike at those roots! Strong beliefs easily lead to intolerance, and tolerance often masks indifference. Either without the other is a counterfeit of authentic discipleship.

For Wesley, conforming to the image of Christ, being made perfect in love, is the test of faith and faithfulness. Love is a more accurate reflection of one's devotion to Christ than the dogmatism of one's beliefs. Wesley considered the failure to love another whose religious beliefs and practices differ from one's own a form of religious bigotry. Rejection and hatred in the name of religion are but pious sins.

Perhaps nothing damages the witness of the Christian church more than our failure to combine strong convictions with tolerance. We have some among us who diligently challenge the church to defend the historic creeds against all threats. They have a legitimate concern. Yet, often the concern is expressed in name-calling, labeling, and downright meanness. The heart of the faith, love, is thereby denied in the process of defending the faith.

On the other hand, some among us use tolerance as an excuse for indifference when it comes to the core doctrines of the church. It is as though beliefs do not matter. Beliefs do matter! Clarifying and proclaiming the church's understanding of the nature, activity, and purposes of God made known in Jesus Christ is an indispensable component of Christian discipleship. Love and convictions are not enemies; they belong together.

Jesus is our model. He was firm in his relationship with and devotion to God, and his relationship to God was expressed in unconditional love for people, even those who rejected the God whom he revealed. May the mind that was in Christ Jesus be in us.

Sin Is Real

A CHARACTER IN ONE OF PETER DEVRIES' SHORT STORIES observes, "There was a time when we were afraid of being caught doing something sinful in front of our ministers. Now we are afraid of being caught doing something immature in front of our therapists."

Thomas Long writes in an issue of *Theology Today*: "Prayers of confession are banished from liturgies as 'too dreary'; sermons on sin are avoided in the name of preserving self-esteem. No one at a government hearing confesses sin. Miscalculations, perhaps. Errors in judgement, maybe. Inconsistencies at this point in time, surely. But sin? Never."

While sin is trivialized and diminished in our vocabulary, its destructive dominance grows within human experience. Our own actions and the daily news contain ample ugly evidence of sin's pervasive presence. Yet we seldom call evil what it is. Mistakes, errors, miscalculations, sickness, immaturity, maladjustment sound more acceptable and less judgmental than sin.

Furthermore, mistakes and miscalculations can be easily corrected. We can grow out of immaturity. Sickness can be treated with a new medication, or surgery, or diet and exercise. Emotional maladjustment can be cured by therapy, a support group, and a better mental outlook.

Please don't get me wrong. Therapy, medicine, support groups and human effort are means of healing, growth, and maturity. They are not, however, cures for sin. Sin is too pervasive and systemic to be removed by science, technology, and human effort. It is more than a flaw in the personality which can be corrected by individual initiative, legislative pronouncements, or therapeutic intervention.

Sin goes to the core of the human condition. Only One who has assumed the human struggle with the power of evil and triumphed over it can conquer sin. The good news is that God has taken the initiative to destroy sin. In the crucifixion of Jesus Christ, God took on the principalities and powers of death and sin and God won! What humanity cannot do on its own behalf, God has done.

Confession and turning away from sin are the appropriate responses to God's victory. Rather than denying, trivializing, or misnaming sin, let us confess it and live in the light of God's victory in Jesus Christ.

Christ's Commands Are Covered

JESUS PLACES HIGH DEMANDS ON DISCIPLES. OBEYING Christ's commands requires more than determination and willpower. None of us can claim total obedience. Living up to Jesus' commands is clearly beyond our ability. Below are but a few of the commands Jesus gave his disciples:

> Love your enemies.
>
> You shall love the Lord your God with all your heart, with all your strength, with all your soul, and with all your mind . . . and you shall love your neighbor as yourself.
>
> You shall be perfect as your Heavenly Father is perfect.
>
> Take up your cross daily and follow me.

John Wesley preached that all the commands of Christ are covered by Christ's promises. That which Christ commands, Christ makes possible. The commands are given in the context of a relationship with us. They are not the preconditions of a relationship. That is, Christ does not promise that he will be with us if we obey. Since he is with us, we can obey. The commands are promises of Christ's faithfulness to us and signs of our obedience to Christ.

How we view Christ's commands makes a difference. When seen as preconditions for discipleship, the commandments are burdensome legalism and impossible standards. However, when seen as promises of what Christ can and will do in us, the commandments become gifts to be accepted and nurtured.

Wesley wrote in a sermon on Christian perfection, ". . . that general and unlimited promise which runs through the whole gospel, 'I will put my laws in their minds, and write them in their heart,' turns all the commands into promises. . . ." He adds, "As he [God] has called us to holiness he is undoubtedly willing, as well as able, to work this holiness in us." Wesley was convinced that Christ will work in us what God requires of us.

Christ's commands are covered by Christ's promises.

THE APOSTLES' CREED IS A
PLEDGE OF ALLEGIANCE

O NE OF THE MOST PROVOCATIVE BOOKS I HAVE READ IN recent months is *Loyalty to God, The Apostles' Creed in Life and Liturgy* by Theodore W. Jennings Jr. It is a commentary on the Apostles' Creed and its place in the life and liturgy of Christians.

Dr. Jennings argues persuasively that the historic Creed functions primarily as an affirmation of loyalty and commitment rather than as a summary of intellectual propositions. Reciting the Creed is a commitment of faithfulness to a particular God. It is more like a pledge of allegiance than a statement of beliefs.

In some contexts, reciting the Creed has been considered a subversive act. It is called a "confession of faith" because it is an admission of loyalty to the God revealed in Jesus Christ above loyalty to lesser gods such as the nation, a particular political or economic system, an ethnic group, or even the family. I suspect that living the Creed in any context is subversive, for it runs counter to the prevailing culture.

Faith has to do more with faithfulness than with mental or verbal assent to theological propositions. Rather than faith being defined as belief in that which cannot be proven, faith is living in terms of God's reality and reign even when God seems hidden and powerless. It is remaining faithful to God even when faithfulness brings no obvious rewards. Faith is doing the will of God even when beliefs about God seem confused and unbelievable. Jesus said, "'Not everyone who says to me, "Lord, Lord," will enter the kingdom of heaven, but only the one who does the will of my Father in heaven'" (Matt. 7:21).

The Apostles' Creed is included in the liturgy of most of our churches. It is more than a routine reciting of memorized theological propositions. It is a pledge of loyalty to God who transforms the world and calls us to live transformed lives.

Part Three

Current Issues

Visiting the Prisoners • Sense and the Senseless • Evil and Goodness Exposed in Oklahoma City • Sabotaging Our Own Ideals • Confronting Profitable Idols • Between Too Much and Too Little • The Church and Racial Barriers • Going to the House across the Street • One Step Toward Overcoming Racism • A Monster Is Loose among Us • Bashing As Political Strategy • Getting "Tough on Crime" Is No Solution • We Are Losing Our Own Children • Biblical Justice and Compassion and Welfare Reform • God's Test of Justice and Righteousness • Position on Gambling • Would Jesus Support the Death Penalty? • A Lesson from the Ants • Is the Church Guilty of Child Neglect? • The Devil Made Me Do It • The Light Shines in the Darkness • But We Should Be Better . . . • Opposing the Legislation Regarding the Ten Commandments • Becoming Monsters While Destroying Monsters • The Militarization of Religion • Violence Is a Religion

Part Three
Current Issues

Visiting the Prisoners

JUDGE FRANK WILSON WAS A FEDERAL district judge in Chattanooga, Tennessee, before his death. He was an active member of the United Methodist Church and a devout Christian. Judge Wilson contacted each person whom he sentenced to prison. During a speech at the Holston Annual Conference session in 1966 or 1967 he said something that changed my ministry. Judge Wilson said, "Pastors should be as familiar with inside the local jails and prisons as they are the hospitals."

The judge's statement indicted me. I had never been inside a jail. It really had not occurred to me to visit the county jail located two miles from the church I served. Hospital visitation was an almost daily routine. Nursing homes were on the schedule to be visited at least once monthly. Of course, church members were in hospitals

65

and nursing homes. Rarely have I had members in jails or prisons.

Immediately upon return from Annual Conference, I made a visit to the Sullivan County Jail. The practice of visiting the jails and prisons continued during my years as a pastor. Some of my most memorable and enriching experiences have occurred during those visits. I naively assumed that I would take God to the prisoners. God always got there first.

I am convinced that John Wesley's visits to England's prisons shaped his life and ministry as much as his visit at Aldersgate Street. He regularly accompanied condemned malefactors to the gallows. The early Methodists would no more neglect visiting the prisoners than attending worship.

The jail and prison populations are mushrooming. At the end of 1994, 1,053,738 people were housed in state and federal prisons— triple the number incarcerated in 1980. Add the number in local jails and we have an astronomical number of people incarcerated in our communities. Almost all jails and prisons have a United Methodist Church nearby. Visiting the jails and prisons in the community is as important as visiting hospitals and nursing homes.

There is One whom we can always count on meeting in prison. Jesus will say, "I was in prison and you visited me" or "I was in prison and you didn't visit."

SENSE AND THE SENSELESS

THE CRUEL BOMBING OF THE FEDERAL BUILDING IN Oklahoma City confronted us again with the tragic consequences of violence. Innocent lives snuffed out, families grieving for dead loved ones, fear and suspicion multiplied, loss of trust and freedom—these are among the rubble of a wanton act of violence.

A rabbi was asked by a reporter: "How do you explain this tragedy?" The rabbi responded something like this: "I don't explain it. It doesn't make sense. It will never make sense. This violence is so senseless that to explain it would be to fit it into the normal. Violence must never be made to seem sensible."

Many attempts have been made to explain why persons would blow up a building crowded with people. Various plausible psychological, social, political reasons have been advanced. Those who committed the atrocity likely have reasons which make sense to them. Commentators, preachers, editorial writers, and politicians have pointed accusing fingers in multiple directions, always away from themselves or ourselves.

The rabbi's comment seems to point in a different direction. Violence makes no sense! Violence is diabolical, sinful, demonic, an affront to God and human decency. Any attempt to justify violence or make sense of it as something other than sin or evil only helps to accommodate it.

Since the dawn of human history, however, violence has been a quick answer to wrong. Evil has been dressed up in the garments of respectability and promoted as a means to self-justified ends and harmless entertainment. The senseless has been rationalized, exploited, marketed, applauded, and domesticated.

We can all understand the depth of the evil. The immediate outcry after the bombing was for the death penalty. Answer violence with violence—that is the world's way. It makes sense!

But, until Jesus' teaching in the Sermon on the Mount and his example on the Cross make sense to us and violence makes no sense, the human family will continue to be torn asunder by violence.

EVIL AND GOODNESS EXPOSED IN OKLAHOMA CITY

THE SENSELESS, BRUTAL, EVIL BOMBING WHICH TOOK PLACE in Oklahoma City exposed the worst and the best in the human spirit. Wanton, deadly violence perpetrated on innocent, unsuspecting people, including little children, reveals the depth and pervasiveness of human sin. The human capacity to do evil seems limitless, and the evil acts of the few bring unimaginable suffering and grief to the many.

Heroism, the selfless risk of one's life to relieve the suffering of others, reveals the breadth and height of human goodness. Medical personnel, rescue workers, ordinary citizens abandoning self-interest and routine concerns in response to the desperate plight of others expresses the often latent impulses to give oneself to acts of compassion and mercy. The human capacity for goodness, love, and courage is boundless; the grace-filled actions of the few bring incalculable comfort and hope to the many.

The tendency is to lodge evil and goodness in distinct persons or groups and assume the depravity of some and the nobility of others. The assumption is that identifying and eliminating the evil ones will make the world safe and good. So, we naturally call for immediate retribution against those labeled as evil.

However, the good and the evil do not seem to be so easily segregated. They coexist within the same persons. Indeed, both dwell within each of us. One who was a terrorist and an apostle wrote: "So I find it to be a law that when I want to do what is good, evil lies close at hand" (Rom. 7:21).

Joseph, who saved Egypt and his own kinfolk from starvation, subsequently enacted the policy of exchange that resulted in the Hebrews being enslaved. The one who freed the Hebrew slaves, Moses, was guilty of murder. The king who established the golden age of Israelite sovereignty, David, betrayed the law of God and the nation. One who gave up everything to follow Jesus, Judas, marked him for execution, and the soldier who put Jesus to death declared him to be "the Son of God."

Knowing the conflict between good and evil which resides within the human spirit, Paul cried out, "Who will rescue me from this body of death?" His response merits our reflection, proclamation, and implementation, "Thanks be to God through Jesus Christ our Lord!" Through the grace of God in Jesus Christ goodness triumphs over evil!

Sabotaging Our Own Ideals

WHILE AWAY FROM HOME A FEW MONTHS AGO, I FOUND A park near the hotel where I could walk. Arriving at the walking track about the same time each day was a man in his mid-thirties. He began exercising by carefully going through the recommended stretching and warm-up routines. He then began the vigorous and strenuous jogging routine. He grunted and huffed around the trail until perspiration dripped from his face. After four laps he left the track, went over to his warm-up jacket and took something from the pocket. He then reentered the track for a final walking lap while smoking a cigarette.

Vigorously exercising the heart and lungs while smoking a cigarette—does that not seem inconsistent? All the sweating and straining to improve one's health while simultaneously doing that which undermines health is an example of a hypocrisy which we all share.

Is that smoking jogger anymore incongruous than:

- Affirming the importance of a strong, vital church but attending only sporadically, giving sparingly, and serving minimally?
- Wanting safe highways and streets while driving under the influence of alcohol or failing to observe speed limits?
- Killing people who kill people in order to protect the sacredness or value of life?
- Singing "This Is My Father's World" while searing the mountains, poisoning the air, and polluting the streams?
- Defending doctrines of the Christian faith with hatred, physical or verbal violence, and self righteousness?
- Proclaiming God's love for all people while holding on to prejudices and destructive discrimination?

Indeed, we tend to be our own worst enemies. Our noble ideals are frequently sabotaged by our own attitudes, choices, and behavior.

CONFRONTING PROFITABLE IDOLS

THE APOSTLE PAUL WAS CHASED OUT OF EPHESUS FOR saying that little silver statues of Artemis were no gods (Acts 19). Those statues had become popular and profitable. In fact, the production of silver images of Artemis had become the economic staple of the city. We can almost hear them argue: "Think how many jobs are going to be lost if people listen to Paul. Even if Artemis is an idol, the statues are good for the economy."

Challenging idols is dangerous business. Idols always generate profit for someone. Nothing is resisted more strenuously than that which threatens financial gain. Communities have been known to tolerate and defend all kinds of activity in the name of protecting jobs, lowering taxes, and enhancing economic security.

Are there modern counterparts to the silver statues of Artemis? Are there destructive gods whose promotion and production continue in the name of economic necessity?

What about tobacco? The government officially labels tobacco a health hazard while subsidizing its production. It is a staple of the economy of some states. Powerful lobbyists argue convincingly that the loss of those little smoking idols will result in lost income.

What about weapons of war? Since the production and sale of military hardware is a significant part of the American economy, the United States has become the largest arms merchant in the world while calling for a reduction of weapons.

What about gambling? How much of the current popular support of gambling is based purely on the superficial argument that it is a source of income for the cities and states. Lottery tickets and poker chips promising quick solutions to financial woes are but profitable idols.

What about the church's temptation to substitute idols of statistical growth for faithfulness to God and the integrity of the gospel? Blunting the prophetic witness, avoiding controversial issues, and neglecting risky mission can be piously rationalized in the name of defending statistically profitable idols.

Perhaps we all share the guilt of the Ephesians. It's impossible to consider any issue apart from vested interest. We must, however, avoid silencing the prophetic voices and resisting the divine purpose in the name of protecting our economic advantages. What does it really profit if the world is gained at the expense of the soul?

BETWEEN TOO MUCH AND TOO LITTLE

BISHOP EMERSON COLAW TELLS OF A PASTOR WHO WAS leading a work project at Red Bird Mission in southern Kentucky. The pastor spent the night in the home of one of the families in the community. The little house was sparsely furnished, containing few conveniences to which the pastor was accustomed. As the pastor went to his bedroom his host said, "Down here we often use the phrase: 'if you want anything we don't have, just ask for it and we'll show you how to get along without it.'"

Many of us remember when current necessities were luxuries: television, indoor plumbing, telephones, air conditioning, central heat, microwave ovens, refrigerators, motorized lawn mowers, computers, word processors, photocopiers, comfortable cars, jet airplanes, diet cola, frozen yogurt, wash and wear clothing. Living without such technological advances is unthinkable to most of us. A temporary power failure or plumbing malfunction creates a major crisis in our households. We are, indeed, addicted to comfort and convenience.

Yet, to millions of our sisters and brothers, adequate food and shelter are only dreamed-of luxuries. While the principal cause of disease and premature death in our country is over consumption of nonessentials, the primary cause of disease and premature death in the so-called Third World is under consumption of necessities. While thousands in our land die from the abuse of the products of our affluence, millions in the world die from lack of protective shelter, nutritious food, clean water, essential medical care, and basic human rights.

I don't know the solution to the growing disparity between those who suffer from too much and those who die from not having enough. But those of us who are among the conspicuous consumers can learn to get along with less and share with those who have little or none. The church offers many avenues for those who have plenty to share with those who exist with little.

THE CHURCH AND RACIAL BARRIERS

A STRIKING INCONGRUITY EXISTS IN OUR CITIES: widespread racial polarization and churches in every neighborhood. The coexistence of racial prejudice and religious faith testifies to the failure of the church to fulfill its mission.

Religious communities exist as signs of God's dream for the world. People of faith are called to live now in the light of the divine dream for all humanity. God dreams of a world in which diverse people live in relationships of mutual goodwill, celebrating their kinship as sisters and brothers. God's purpose, therefore, includes the removal of barriers which separate human beings.

In God's dream world, differences are celebrated and nurtured as gifts which enrich the human family. As creatures made in the image of their Creator, the human family expresses the richness and depth of God's own being. Racial hostility, prejudice, and violence turn God's dream into a nightmare. When differences result in hatred and injustice, the creatures distort the image of their Creator and thwart the divine purpose for humanity. Racial prejudice and hostility are signs of a community off course.

Churches are to serve as beacons of reconciliation, justice, and peace as they live out God's vision for humanity. Mutual respect and love rooted in divine love for all people should characterize every church in every neighborhood. Differences are to be accepted as grace-filled gifts and manifestations of the Divine Spirit.

One of the great tragedies is that faith in God, which should remove barriers and solidify the human family, is a major contributor to the world's hatred and violence. Religious communities often reflect and promote God's nightmare more than they reveal God's dream. Homogeneity characterizes most congregations and racial diversity is a rare site on Sunday morning. Rather than countering racial polarization and bitterness, churches thereby acquiesce to prevailing divisions and separation.

The existence of racial polarization in a city with a church in every neighborhood is cause for repentance and hope. As we repent of our unfaithfulness to God's dream we can turn and live toward that dream.

GOING TO THE HOUSE ACROSS THE STREET

SOMETIME AGO I JOINED A WORK TEAM THAT WAS rehabilitating a church building located in an economically depressed neighborhood. Twenty-five or thirty persons had come into the city from suburban churches to paint, repair, and refurbish a church building surrounded by unkempt houses and marginalized people.

I noticed two youngsters playing in the lawn across the street. They seemed curious about all the strangers busily painting, mowing, raking, hammering, and sawing in their neighborhood. I wandered across the road, stood at the fence, and struck up a conversation with the boys, aged about seven and nine. I asked if they go to church anywhere. One said, "no," and the other replied that his uncle "takes me sometime." I told them about the after school program each day at the church across the street and suggested they might want to try it.

After about twenty minutes, I rejoined my colleagues at the church. One worker, familiar with the neighborhood, humorously chided me about "going to the house across the street." She said, "After all, we suspect that is a house of prostitution."

I have thought a lot about that incident. It says some things about us that concern me. For one thing, we are more comfortable rehabilitating buildings than rehabilitating lives. Painting and mowing come easier to most of us than relating to people whose values and behavior run contrary to ours. Working on structures alongside like-minded colleagues comes more naturally than sharing the gospel with the alienated, exploited, and outcast people.

Also, the incident raised anew for me the question: Why does the church exist? Why repair and refurbish a building if it doesn't serve the neighborhood? This particular church does serve the community through tutoring, feeding, and counseling its neighbors, and it does so with few resources. But many church buildings stand idle and inaccessible while surrounded by children, youth, and adults who desperately need the fellowship and ministry of a community of grace.

Perhaps the test of our faithfulness as a church is our willingness to share the gospel with "the house across the street." After all, the church is about restoring the divine image in persons, not refurbishing and maintaining buildings inaccessible to the poor, the despised, and the neglected.

ONE STEP TOWARD OVERCOMING RACISM

RACISM SEEMS TO BE INTENSIFYING AROUND THE WORLD. "Ethnic cleansing" is a new name for an old sin, the practice of ridding our world, our neighborhood, our church, our circle of friendships, of the people who are different. Exclusion assumes the inherent superiority of one's own group and the desirability of defending its "purity."

Separation based upon race perpetuates racism. Although discrimination in housing is unlawful, most of us live in communities filled with our own kind of people. And, the church probably remains the most segregated institution in our society.

A tragedy of segregation is the difficulty of forming friendships across lines of race and ethnicity. I was an adult before I had an African-American friend. What a loss for me! Failure to understand, respect, and appreciate the unique gifts and cultural backgrounds of others impoverishes us all.

As a sign, foretaste, and instrument of the reign of God, the church is to bring members of God's family together. Racism in the church is a sin against God and a betrayal of the church's nature and mission. Rejection of a person, including a pastor, because of race is a denial of Jesus Christ in whom "there is no longer Jew or Greek, there is no longer slave or free, there is no longer male and female; for all of you are one in Christ Jesus" (Gal. 3:28). We simply cannot accept Jesus Christ as Lord and Savior and hate or make invisible the persons for whom he died.

The district superintendents and I have entered into a covenant with one another to form listening and friendship ties with members of other races. We will be intentional in confronting our own prejudices and in holding one another accountable for overcoming that which separates us from our brothers and sisters.

Forming caring relationships with persons of a different race is not the final answer to racism. It is, however, a requirement of the gospel and an indispensable component of the church's nature and mission.

A Monster Is Loose among Us

A MONSTER IS ON THE RAMPAGE IN OUR SOCIETY. IT appears with increasing frequency in every community. Its victims include persons of all ages, from little babies to robust youth to defenseless grandparents.

The monster's name is *Violence*. Although it comes in various disguises, the violence monster is always ugly; and it leaves a wake of tears and trauma wherever it appears.

Nobody seems to know the exact origin of this brutal monster. Psychologists speculate that such experiences as the deprivation of love, poor self-image, and early encounters with rejection help to create the monster. Sociologists point to such social ills as poverty, discrimination, loss of family cohesiveness, unemployment, and drug and alcohol abuse as monster creators. Preachers say that sin, despair, and hopelessness give birth to the violence monster.

They are all correct. The violence monster is birthed and nurtured from a multitude of sources. And the truth is, there is some of the monster in all of us. Aggressiveness and anger live within each human personality, and with proper taming, they become contributors to human good rather than destroyers of life itself.

The violence monster uses many weapons. Guns and knives, clubs and fists, bombs and bullets are obvious favorites. More subtle violence monsters use words and manipulations. The eyes and tongues and pen can be deadly weapons.

Some fundamental changes are needed in our values and attitudes. As long as violence is a form of entertainment and a primary means of settling differences and defending self-interest, the violence monster will get bigger and more deadly.

Respect and reverence for all life as a gift from God, acceptance of differences, willingness to dialogue, love for all persons, including enemies—these are attitudes and values which eliminate violence.

The place to begin is with the potential violence monsters that live within our own personalities and within those whom we nurture and influence.

Bashing As Political Strategy

IS IT ONLY MY PERCEPTION OR HAS BASHING BECOME THE principal strategy in the current political campaigns? I am having considerable difficulty determining where candidates really stand on issues. The aspirants to state and national offices seem more preoccupied with diminishing their opponents than illumining their own positions. One newspaper report said that the races will be determined by the "negative" image of the competitor, not the quality of the victor.

That is a disturbing commentary on the state of public discourse. For the leadership of any institution, including the church, to be determined by one's effectiveness in making opponents look bad is a dangerous omen. Character assassination by innuendo and personal attacks replace clarification of issues, articulation of vision, and maintenance of personal integrity. The result is manipulation, lost vision, and compromised ethics.

Educating the electorate on substantive issues confronting the state and nation are risky, but desperately needed, strategies. Critically important matters such as crime, health care, tax and welfare reform, public education, housing, and the collapse of community are being treated with slogans and personal attacks. Television political ads consist mostly of bashing opponents with cleverly designed, misleading, and sometimes dishonest sound bites and images.

I have to admit that bashing frequently shows up in the church. It is nearly impossible to have a productive discussion of such critical issues as language for God, the meaning of the incarnation and the atonement, the inclusiveness of the church, homosexuality, abortion, capital punishment, etc. The issues have become so politicized that labeling has replaced listening and destroying opponents has become more urgent than living the kingdom life.

When bashing becomes a dominant political strategy in the society and/or the church, both society and the church are in jeopardy. May God help us all to rise above bashing.

GETTING "TOUGH ON CRIME" IS NO SOLUTION

F EAR OF CRIME IS INCREASING AS VIOLENCE AND THEFT spread into all neighborhoods. Crime is a serious problem and it merits concern and response by all institutions, including the church.

The popular solution offered by persons running for public office is to "get tough on crime" by putting offenders in prison for longer periods of time and by executing more murderers. In other words, imprisonment and capital punishment are supposed to reduce crime and violence.

Unfortunately, "get tough" proposals ignore the causes of crime and they merely express our anger and fear. Bigger prisons and more executions will not make our streets and neighborhoods safer. They likely will only intensify the problem while increasing the cost to taxpayers.

If prisons reduced crime, the United States would have one of the lowest crime rates in the world. However, the U.S. currently leads the western world in percentage of citizens in prison, the rate of crime, and the length of prison sentences.

And, if capital punishment were a deterrent, most offenses would have been eliminated in King George III's England. More than two hundred offenses were punishable by hanging. One capital offense was picking pockets. A place where persons were most likely to have their pockets picked was the public hanging of pickpockets. Almost invariably the states which execute the most people have the highest murder rate. Executions cheapen life, play on the lowest human motivations, diminish humanity, and they run contrary to the teaching and example of Jesus who was an innocent victim of a government-sanctioned execution.

Churches can contribute to the solution to crime and violence by:

- teaching by precept and example love for God and neighbor as the supreme law of life
- incorporating into the fellowship the outsider, the lonely, the alienated
- treating all children and youth as "our children" who need love and care
- working to eliminate poverty, racism, and all forms of injustice
- supporting strong educational, health, recreational, and other community oriented institutions
- demonstrating alternatives to verbal and physical violence as solutions to conflict
- challenging popular non-solutions such as "get tough" and capital punishment
- visit those who are in prison, as commanded by Jesus and practiced by the early Methodists

The most promising solution to crime and violence is for the church to be the church, the community of Christ!

WE ARE LOSING OUR OWN CHILDREN

T HE POPULAR NOTION IS THAT THE MEMBERSHIP DECLINE in the United Methodist Church results from our members transferring to other denominations, especially more conservative ones. The fact is, many more people transfer to the United Methodist Church than transfer from it to other denominations.

A major factor in the membership decline is our failure to persuade our own children of the power and validity of the gospel. We are losing our own children and youth, not to other churches but to no church. Each year we lose almost twice as many members by death and "Charge Conference Action" as we receive on profession of faith and confirmation.

Children are at great risk in our society. Violence by and against children is rampant. The majority of the world's poor are children, and the number of aborted and unwanted children continues to increase. It appears that children are increasingly considered to be disposable. Jessica DeBoer (or is she now Anna Schmidt?) and Kimberly Mays have come to symbolize adults' property rights more than kids' human rights.

But what about the church's neglect of children and our failure as adults to pass on the faith story to our children? Is that not a form of child neglect? Maybe we are putting children at risk by failing to be their advocates, friends, defenders, teachers.

Every local church I served had trouble recruiting Sunday School teachers, especially those who would commit to long-term relationships with kids. And, too many church leaders have been more protective of their classroom walls and waxed floors than they have been concerned for the children's physical, emotional, and spiritual well-being.

I heard recently of a board of trustees that tried to keep the neighborhood kids off the church steps. The pastor decided to join the children on the steps where she told them Bible stories. Soon the children were coming inside, even on Sunday morning. Now the church is growing!

We must practice what Jesus preached and practiced: "'. . . Let the little children come to me, and do not stop them . . .'" (Matt. 19:14). Failure to do so is a form of child abuse.

BIBLICAL JUSTICE AND COMPASSION AND WELFARE REFORM

IN THE BIBLE, JUSTICE AND COMPASSION ARE NOT LEGAL terms or emotions. They are actions toward and relationship with the most vulnerable people of the community. Justice isn't the impartial balancing of an imaginary scale. It is deliberate and generous aid to "the fatherless, the widow, the stranger." Compassion is specific action toward those in need, not a subjective feeling. The Bible's criteria for determining justice and compassion is this: Does it protect the weakest members of the community and promote their well-being?

John Wesley believed that the Bible requires every action and decision be evaluated by the impact on the least, weakest, and most vulnerable. Religion, according to Wesley, must go from the weak to the powerful rather than the reverse. Justice and compassion begin with the weak and vulnerable or they do not meet the test of God's righteousness. Any proposal that ignores the plight of the poor and vulnerable lacks God's justice and compassion.

Absent from current discussions of welfare reform are biblical justice and compassion. Cutting assistance and removing the safety net is neglect, not reform. Block grant proposals sound more like a Pilate-style hand washing than a striving for justice and compassion.

The present welfare system, though well-intentioned, destroys the values it seeks to create. It must be reformed. However, the "block grant" and cutback plans being offered in Congress adversely impact the most vulnerable, especially impoverished children. They fail the biblical test of justice and compassion.

Both the United Methodist Church and the United States government have failed to live up to the Bible's mandate to practice justice and compassion. The current welfare system and the legislative proposals to reform it both reflect the destructive consequences of our failure to practice what the Bible preaches about God's reign of justice, generosity, and joy.

Repentance of our failure means turning toward God's justice and compassion. Authentic welfare reform must begin with the impoverished children, not with the cost to middle-class and affluent taxpayers. Repentance requires that the church put the poor, the imprisoned, the sick, the outcast, the marginalized at the center of its life and mission.

GOD'S TEST OF JUSTICE AND RIGHTEOUSNESS

THE FOLLOWING IS THE THEOLOGICAL TEST OF JUSTICE and righteousness: What is the impact on the weakest and most vulnerable persons? The Bible is unambiguous and clear. From God's choice and deliverance of the Hebrew slaves to God's incarnation in a defenseless baby and a crucified Savior, God has demonstrated a redemptive bias on behalf of the poor, the outcasts, the outsiders.

Jesus declared that responsiveness to "the least of these" is inseparable from responsiveness to God (Matt. 25:31–46). He equated the receiving of a little child with receiving him (Mark 9:36–37), and he warned of grave consequences to those who caused "little ones" to sin (Matt. 18:6). The Epistle of James defines true religion as caring for the fatherless and the widow and giving preferential attention to the poor (James 1:26, 2:1–6).

What if the impact on "the least of these," especially the children, were to become the criteria by which all decisions were made by both the government and the church? How would "The First Hundred Days" of the current Congress fare if evaluated on the basis of the Bible's understanding of justice and righteousness? It appears that the legislation passed by the House of Representatives will have the most immediate adverse impact on poor children.

What is the church doing to implement justice and righteousness? We, too, must evaluate everything we do in terms of the impact on the most vulnerable, especially the children. Almost every church is surrounded by neighborhoods filled with children. Yet, in too many of our churches, the children are conspicuous by their absence. Too many of our church buildings are vacant at times when they could be filled with children attending after school programs, recreational activities, preschool care, and tutoring opportunities. Low-income housing projects are crowded with children who would gladly attend our Sunday Schools if we would only provide transportation, adult relationships, and warm hospitality.

Judged by the Bible's understanding of justice and righteousness, both the nation and the church fall sinfully short. Repentance and turning with compassion toward those for whom God has a bias is the mandate of the gospel. A good place to begin is with the children.

POSITION ON GAMBLING

SINCE THE TENNESSEE LEGISLATURE IS CONSIDERING A constitutional amendment to permit a referendum on legalizing gambling, it seems appropriate to state the position of the United Methodist Church. The following is a quote from the Social Principles:

> Gambling is a menace to society, deadly to the best interests of moral, social, economic, and spiritual life, and destructive of good government. As an act of faith and love, Christians should abstain from gambling, and should strive to minister to those victimized by the practice. Community standards and personal life-styles should be such as would make unnecessary and undesirable the resort to commercial gambling, including public lotteries, as a recreation, as an escape, or as a means of producing public revenue or funds for support of charities or government. (1992 *Discipline*, p. 101f)

Gambling exploits the poor and fosters greed by promising effortless financial reward. As a means of raising revenue it enables governments to avoid the substantive issue of appropriate taxation necessary for adequate funding of needed services.

The promise of getting something for nothing appeals to most of us. Becoming a millionaire by buying a lottery ticket or returning a sweepstakes ticket seems easy and harmless. Yet, such a promise undermines basic ethical principles of justice, compassion, and personal initiative.

Governments exist to provide services to their people by promoting the common good. Funding needed services through state-sponsored gambling makes the government an accomplice to disservice. Gambling infects the soul of individuals and communities. It is no solution to budgetary woes, and any immediate benefits are more than offset by long-term liabilities.

Gambling that gambling is a solution to any problem is indeed a foolish and dangerous gamble.

WOULD JESUS SUPPORT THE DEATH PENALTY?

THE CURRENT CLAMOR FOR THE DEATH PENALTY represents a frightening commentary on our society. The politically popular call for the speedy execution of murderers is an appalling sign of moral insensitivity and an example of the dangerous exploitation of fear, frustration, and prejudice.

No studies anywhere in the world support the claim that the death penalty is a deterrent to violence. Historically the states that execute people for murder have the highest rates of murder. Furthermore, the death penalty, as used in the United States, discriminates against the poor and ethnic minorities. The two common characteristics of those sentenced to death are: (1) they are poor and were represented by court-appointed attorneys, and (2) their victims were white. In fact, of the more than 18,700 people executed in this country since 1608, only 31 killed black persons. And, a disproportionate number on death row are African-Americans and Hispanics.

Many Christians support capital punishment by citing Scripture. There are Old Testament passages which call for the sentence of death. But if those passages are the basis for executions, then the crimes for which we are justified in putting people to death include blasphemy, talking back to one's parents, and adultery.

As Christians we are guided by the teachings of Jesus and the model of his life and mission. Our reference is to and from him.

Therefore, the basis for my strong opposition to the death penalty is this question: "Would Jesus pull the switch on the electric chair?" Jesus warned against vengeance. He was the victim of the death penalty and he died with a prayer of forgiveness on his lips. He taught and lived a love which transcends "an eye for an eye."

I have concluded that Jesus would never sanction the death penalty. He knew that violence breeds violence, that love is stronger than death, that reconciliation and transformation are always possible, and that vengeance belongs to God.

Jesus would not pull the switch, so neither should we.

A LESSON FROM THE ANTS

DR. CHARLES RAY GOFF, WHO WAS PASTOR OF CHICAGO Temple several years ago, tells in one of his sermons about kicking an ant hill that had been built in his lawn. He totally shattered the dirt home of the ants. He assumed that he had permanently robbed the ants of their city.

Instead of scampering away in fear and despair or calling a meeting to plan for a new home, each ant began grabbing the nearest lump of dirt and started pulling it back into location. Within a few hours the ants had completely rebuilt their city. They did it with a lump of dirt at a time and with each ant carrying what seemed to be more than its share of the load.

Many overwhelming problems exist in our world. It is as though reckless and cruel intruders are plummeting civilization into an abyss. The environment is threatened with poison and depletion. Nations and ethnic groups seek to destroy one another. Violence stalks our cities. Hunger and starvation threaten millions of our brothers and sisters. Drug and alcohol abuse destroys minds and bodies. Sin is alive and thriving.

Giving up in despair seems to be a reasonable response. After all, our resources are limited. What can one person, or one church, do against such overwhelming odds?

Part of the answer, however, lies with people taking hold where they are and working, piece by piece, for a better world. A piece of the solution to every problem which plagues our world is within our reach.

We may not be able to remove all violence, hatred, starvation, addiction, injustice, and evil. But each person, each congregation can do something. After all, there is more at work in the world than our own efforts. It is amazing what God does with even a little faithfulness.

God's dream of a new world, though shattered by the evil and carelessness of the human family, will be put in place a piece at a time. May we as individuals and congregations shoulder our share of the load.

Is the Church Guilty of Child Neglect?

WE WERE ALL HORRIFIED AND ANGERED BY THE DEATHS OF the two little boys in McMinnville whose mother left them in a hot car while she partied and slept in a motel room. The public has called for severe punishment of the negligent and preoccupied mother. The public anger is understandable and the neglect of the children is inexcusable.

Literally millions of children die everyday from neglect and abuse. Approximately thirty-five thousand children die of hunger and malnutrition every day. More than one hundred million children have died of poverty-related causes within the last ten years. More than one fourth of the kids who live in American cities are impoverished. Twelve million of the world's children are growing up homeless. Some eighty million children between the ages of ten and fourteen work for low wages in often dangerous conditions to produce less expensive products to be consumed by affluent nations.

Children have become primary victims of violence throughout the world. More children than soldiers now die from war. Wars have slaughtered two million kids and wounded four million during the last fifteen years. Homicide is now the third leading cause of death among children in the United States. A child is killed by gunfire in the U.S. every two hours. An American child is reported abused or neglected in every eleven seconds. More kids were reported abused or neglected in Memphis last year than were reported in all the Sunday Schools in all the churches in both the Tennessee and Memphis Conferences.

While the world's children are dying from hunger, malnutrition, violence and abuse, the church tends to be preoccupied with its own interest. As a denomination the United Methodist Church seems to be more preoccupied with its own institutional survival than the survival of the world's children. We worry more about doctrinal purity than the slaughter of the innocent ones. Preserving the cleanliness of our church walls often seems more important than communicating the God-given worth of every child. Many church folks spend more time in the church gym shaping their bodies after the image of Jane Fonda or Michael Jordan than they spend in the neighborhoods helping to shape lives after the image of Jesus Christ.

Based upon the church's preoccupation and narcissistic self-concern, God has sufficient evidence to convict the United Methodist Church with child neglect and abuse. Greatness, according to Jesus in Luke's Gospel, is measured by how the little children are received. It is clear from the New Testament that we cannot love Jesus and neglect "the little ones."

The mother in McMinnville never intended to let her children die. Her tragic preoccupation resulted in her sons' deaths. May the plight of the world's children awaken the church from its slumber and its neglect of the little ones with whom Jesus lives and dies.

THE DEVIL MADE ME DO IT

THE COMEDIAN FLIP WILSON USED TO JUSTIFY HIS NAUGHTY behavior by saying, "The devil made me do it." He blamed such things as pranks, flirtation, and over indulgence in food or drink on the devil. His devil-motivated action caused folks more embarrassment than real harm. One could get the impression that the devil is a comic prankster, not a destroyer of life.

The irony is that really tragic events are explained not by "The devil made me do it" but by "God told me to do it," or "It's the will of God." God, not the devil, is credited with much of the world's suffering and tragedy. One could get the impression that God is a sadistic despot, not the source of love and life.

Yigal Amir confessed to killing Yitzhak Rabin. He told an Israeli court, "All I did I did for the glory of God." Murder in the name of

God? Slaughter in the name of God is biblical. After all, did not God order the deaths of Canaanite women and children during the Hebrew conquest of the Promised Land? First Samuel contains this haunting statement: ". . . And Samuel hewed Agag in pieces before the Lord in Gilgal" (15:33). Chopping someone in pieces "for the glory of God"? Is God a champion of torture and death?

History bears witness to the devil's effectiveness in using religion as motivation for terrible evil. Wooing and prodding people to do ungodly things under the illusion of obeying God is the devil's most effective seduction. Calling evil good and good evil is the tempter's primary method. Distorting God's nature and purposes is the devil's persistent occupation.

Jesus confronted Satan's seductive attempts to distort God's character and purposes. Jesus, however, refused to practice coercion, manipulation, and political dominance in the name of obedience to God (Matt. 4:1–11). As the incarnation of God, Jesus scorned violence and cruelty even when he was its innocent victim.

Only that which reflects Christlike love glorifies God. Hate, violence, and destruction reflect the demonic, especially when they are done in the name of God. Kindness, compassion, mercy, justice, and integrity qualify as being "for the glory of God."

THE LIGHT SHINES IN THE DARKNESS

THE STORY WAS TOLD BY THE GREAT THEOLOGIAN PAUL Tillich. In the worst days of the massacres in Poland during the Nazi occupation, a young pregnant Jewish woman took refuge in a cemetery. On a bitter cold winter night, she crept into an open grave and gave birth to a son. The next morning the old Jewish gravedigger discovered them. He fell on his knees and cried, "Surely the Messiah has come! Only the Messiah could be born in a grave!" The old gravedigger was doomed to disappointment, for the child died shortly after being born. However, the insight is profound and timeless. It expresses the meaning of Christmas. Only the Messiah could be born in a grave!

The Gospel writers tell the story of Jesus' birth with stark realism. Luke describes the Messiah's birth as taking place in a stable following a long, dangerous journey. Matthew's portrayal includes the story of Herod's slaughter of the innocent baby boys and the holy family's flight into exile in Egypt. John's account is couched in the language of philosophy and metaphor, but the starkness is there. He writes: "The light shines in the darkness."

We have removed the realism from the Christmas story. Decorations and festivities mask, temporarily at least, the ambiguities of our daily lives. Beneath the gaiety and laughter, however, lurks loneliness and grief, danger and dread. Death and tragedy do not take Christmas vacations. Painful memories and haunting fears almost always push their way into our Christmas experiences.

The world's problems hang on every Christmas. Violence takes more victims. The suicide rate increases. Hunger and homelessness abound. Thousands of innocent children will die of poverty on Christmas Day. While many kids awake to an abundance of gifts, scarcity will keep others asleep permanently. While many families greet one another with warm affection, others will be torn asunder by abuse and neglect.

The good news is this: God has come into the real world! There is no night so dark but what the light still shines! No place is so barren that it does not cradle the divine presence! No person is beyond the reach of God's love. No one is so vulnerable but what she or he can be a channel of transcendent grace. God has claimed all of life as the domain of the divine presence.

Hear again John's resounding affirmation: "The light shines in the darkness and the darkness cannot overcome it!" Thanks be to God!

BUT WE SHOULD BE BETTER . . .

A RECENT SEGMENT ON THE EVENING NEWS INCLUDED AN interview with a former warden of a Mississippi prison. His duties included the supervision of executions. As a result of putting people to death, the warden has become an opponent of capital punishment. He gave two impressive arguments. Both are rooted in his faith and values.

The warden said that he began to wonder if his wife and children were proud of him. Is executing people something that would cause my family to be proud of me? That was a question that haunted him. He added, "And what does my God think of me?"

Further, the warden emphasized that his opposition to the death penalty did not reduce the seriousness of the crimes committed by those sentenced to death. He acknowledged that many of them are terribly dangerous and vicious people who must be kept away from society. "But we should be better than they are," the courageous former warden affirmed. Executing killers only makes killers of executioners.

What our family and God think are important indicators of decency and morality. Anything that brings shame and embarrassment to those we love merits careful scrutiny before doing it. What will be God's response: "Well done, good and faithful servant?" or "As you have done to one of these you have done unto me?" I find it impossible to imagine the God whose Son received the death penalty being proud of state-sanctioned executions.

Jesus rejected "an eye for an eye" as an adequate ethical principle. He replaced vengeance and retribution with active goodness. Overcoming evil with good is the Christlike response. Opposition to the death penalty is not sentimentalism or passivity in the presence of meanness. It is the recognition that we should be better than the cruelty we claim to be punishing.

OPPOSING THE LEGISLATION REGARDING THE TEN COMMANDMENTS

I T IS DIFFICULT TO UNDERSTAND HOW TO EXPRESS opposition to legislation calling for posting the Ten Commandments in schools and other public buildings without being against the Ten Commandments. It is precisely my belief in the Commandments that I have expressed opposition to the legislation.

The following is an excerpt from a letter that I sent to several Tennessee legislators:

I wish to express my opposition to the legislative proposal regarding the Ten Commandments. Although I strongly support efforts to strengthen moral and ethical foundations and protect the religious freedom of our citizens, the proposal currently before the General Assembly weakens the religious foundation for morality and undermines religious freedom.

The Ten Commandments are the foundation of ethics and morality in the Judeo-Christian tradition. They have been preached as such for more than three thousand years, and they merit continued proclamation. The Ten Commandments, however, cannot be separated from their theological context in a particular religious community and tradition. The Commandments are in the context of God's covenant with the Hebrew people and begin with these words, "I am the Lord your God, who brought you out of Egypt, out of the land of slavery." Then follows the first Commandment, "You shall have no other gods before me" (Exod. 20:2–3 NIV). It is clearly the God of the Hebrews on whom the Commandments depend.

To require that the Ten Commandments be posted in schools as mere codes of ethics severs them from their historical and theological roots. By reducing them to a secular code of ethics, the Ten Commandments are weakened and even trivialized. It is my understanding that the power of the Commandments lies in the covenant with God who makes obeying them possible. Separating the Ten Commandments from the God who gave them to a covenant community distorts their meaning and robs them of their power. For the state to treat them as a secular code of ethics, therefore, undermines the theological foundation of the Ten Commandments and clearly violates their intent and the intent of the Constitution.

Churches need to preach and teach the Ten Commandments as the gift of the God who liberates from captivity and who enters into covenant with us. To imply that the Commandments are suggested codes of conduct instead of affirmations of faith in and covenant with the God of the Exodus is to diminish them in the name of elevating them.

Becoming Monsters While Destroying Monsters

A GERMAN PHILOSOPHER ONCE ASKED, "OF WHAT VALUE IS it to destroy a monster if you become a monster in the process?" The question merits serious consideration because we church folks often deny the faith in the name of defending it. The philosopher's question warns of the subtle temptation to take on the nature of that which is opposed. We have a tendency to worship the very gods we oppose:

- to become evil while attempting to destroy evil
- to hate those with whom we differ
- to become bigoted toward bigots
- to kill people who kill people to teach reverence for life
- to defend orthodoxy with an unchristian mean spirit
- to self-righteously champion righteousness
- to seek justice by unjust methods
- to build up one's own cause by tearing down another
- to talk of faith while manipulating fear
- to behave heretically while resisting heresy

Jesus and Paul warned of the danger of becoming monsters while destroying monsters. The Sermon on the Mount calls for an inner goodness that remains good while opposing evil. Paul admonished the Roman Christians: "Do not be overcome by evil, but overcome evil with good."

Evil is effectively countered only by goodness. Hate can only be destroyed by love. Violence can only be eliminated by unquenchable goodwill. Vengeance is best defeated by forgiveness. Faith is defended more by faithful living than by forceful argument. Heretical ideas are rendered powerless by grace-shaped persons.

Opposing evil, hate, violence, cruelty, injustice, and heresy can be dangerous and risky. Among the pitfalls is the temptation to become a monster in the process of destroying monsters. Avoiding such a fatal trap requires that we acknowledge that we all stand under the judgment and grace of God.

THE MILITARIZATION OF RELIGION

WORLD EVENTS DEMONSTRATE THE ENORMOUS POWER of religious faith. Regrettably, many modern tragedies have resulted from religious fervor gone mad. Innocent hostages seized, wars between ethnic groups, innocent travelers killed by bomb blasts—these are some of the grotesque acts done in recent years in the name of religion. Holy wars didn't go out with the Middle Ages; they have, in fact, become more deadly.

I flinch every time I read religion being used as adjectives for perpetrators of terrorism, violence, and death—"Christian militia," "Catholic guerrillas," "Protestant army," "Sikh terrorists," "Shiite hijackers," "Jewish captors." Surely such usage of religion is blasphemy of the worst kind.

Hatred is an expression of worship for many. Violence and terrorism are seen as acts of pious devotion. Grenades, rocket launchers, and automatic rifles are treated with the reverence of a religious symbol.

The militarization of religion is one of the most frightening omens in any age. No violent force is quite as powerful as the conviction that it is divinely sanctioned. Adolf Hitler wrote in *Mein Kamph*: "Hence today I believe that I am acting in accordance with the will of the Almighty Creator; by defending myself against the Jew, I am fighting for the work of the Lord."

The ancient Hebrews slaughtered Canaanite men, women, children and even cattle in the name of Yahweh. Christians marched even children off on holy, deadly crusades to conquer the heathen for Christ. Men covered with white sheets gathered on hillsides to pray in the name of Jesus before striking out into their nights of terror against African-Americans.

People who are certain that their every action is in accordance with the divine law aren't likely to be restrained by guilt or reason. Violence and hatred are transformed into virtues when they are perceived as being sanctioned by the Almighty.

When religion motivates hatred, sanctions wanton violence, perpetrates terrorism, and promotes exploitation, it is an instrument of the demonic, whether it is labeled as Christian, Muslim, Jewish, Hindu, or Buddhist.

When religion motivates love, sanctions reconciliation, creates goodwill, and promotes justice, it is an instrument of the divine. As the poet Whittier wrote: "To worship rightly is to love each other."

Current events demonstrate the potency of religious faith. Would to God that the power be manifested in the pursuit of peace among the nations, feeding the world's starving masses, overcoming all forms of injustice, violence, and greed!

May God save us from the militarization of religion!

VIOLENCE IS A RELIGION

WALTER WINK, ONE OF TODAY'S MOST RESPECTED biblical scholars calls violence "the spirituality of the modern world." He writes, "Violence is the ethos of our times. . . . Violence is accorded the status of a religion, demanding from its devotees an absolute obedience-unto-death."

Judged by the homicide rate, the United States is the most violent nation in the industrialized world. Our nation's murder rate, thirty-seven out of one hundred thousand persons, is almost ten times higher than any other country in the Western world. The rate has increased by almost 70 percent during the last eight years. Violence is now a leading cause of death of American children.

Violence has many characteristics of a religion. It is rooted in such basic beliefs as these: might makes right, weapons of violence are sources of security, invincibility is the ultimate power, retribution brings honor and justice, and self-worth is achieved through coercive power. Violence has its sacred symbols and sacred texts—guns and the Constitutional "right to bear arms." The National Rifle Association and the self-styled militia with their rituals of belonging, their claims to be patriotic defenders of freedom, and the demands for conformity and obedience to their creeds function as religious communities.

The basic assumptions which support violence contradict the Christian faith. Jesus warned that "those who live by the sword die by the sword." He taught and practiced an aggressive nonviolence that defines magnanimity and love as the only authentic power. Vulnerability and reliance upon the reign of God are the means to security and self-worth. Only communities that define justice in terms of what happens to "the least of these" are genuine communities.

The destructive reflexes that propagate violence are deep within the human psyche. We who are part of the church are not immune from the idolatry of violence. Prevention and healing begin with the repentance of our own tendency toward violence. Then, we must work to build communities that offer alternatives to retribution and the devilish notions that "might makes right" and vengeance bestows honor. We need to celebrate nonviolence and make heroes of those who practice forgiveness and magnanimity.

The best counter to the religion of violence is the religion of Jesus, who countered the violence visited upon him with a prayer, "Father, forgive them for they know not what they do."

Part Four

Special Topics

Shaped by Worship of the God of Exodus and Jesus • Let Us Pray! • Economism—The Modern World's God • Everybody's Presence Matters • More Than Forgiveness • On Being Aware of the Twilight • It Is Easy to Become What We Hate • "Thank You" Isn't Always Gratitude • The Most Neglected Spiritual Discipline • It's the Perspective That Counts • Finding Our Moral Rudder • The Religious Ignorance Explosion • Gratitude—More Than Counting Blessings • Can We Talk about Values, Meaning, and Faith? • The Tough Mind and the Tender Heart • Jesus Is Rejected in His Hometown • We Need Bouquets and Cabbages • Christians Have Problems Too • Sin Is to Be Forgiven, Not Forgotten • Let Us Confess Our Sins • Winning Is Helping Others to Finish • What Is Success? • A God Who Is Steadfast • Goodness Goes Beyond Mere Obedience • Pious Profanity • We Need to Talk to, Not about • Temptations of Success • The Entrenched Mind • Who Are the Winners? • Two Kinds of Hypocrisy • God Chooses Dreamers • Levels of Love • Happiness Is a False God • Let Us Test the Spirits • Gratitude Springs from Grace • Faith Is More Than Positive Thinking • Judged by Our Judgments • Prayer Is More Than Ceremonial • A Springtime Walk and Worship • On Being Patriotic • Speaking the Truth in Love • He Set His Face to Go to Jerusalem • The Best of All Is, God Is with Us

Part Four
Special Topics

SHAPED BY WORSHIP OF THE GOD OF EXODUS AND JESUS

THE GODS WE WORSHIP SHAPE US AND THE gods that shape us aren't necessarily the God who summons us to worship. Worship means to declare worth or to ascribe worthiness. Whatever we declare as worthy of our allegiance is our god. Whatever shapes and molds us, whatever pulls and pushes us to be and to do is our god. The value or person or vision or thing around which our lives are centered and shaped is our deity.

The church's worship declares the worthiness, celebrates the presence, and reveals the purposes of the God of the Exodus and of Jesus Christ. Corporate Christian worship is a participation in the unfolding of the story of God's grace-filled presence, God's liberating and saving action, and God's final victory over sin and death.

Much worship in the contemporary church, however, declares the worth of the popular gods of success, institutional pragmatism, and personal gratification. The services are designed to attract the religious consumer, bolster the institution's statistical ratings, and satisfy the felt needs of the participants. A result is the trivializing of the transcendent, the profaning of the profound, and the domesticating of the divine.

The Bible is clear. God isn't neutral toward worship. God even "despises" worship that is unconnected to deeds of justice and compassion (Amos 5). Justice and compassion are the true acts of worship of the God who frees the captives and announces good news to the poor. The service of worship in the sanctuary must connect with acts of justice in the world; otherwise, the liturgy becomes a form of blasphemy.

The crisis of worship in the contemporary church has little to do with the nature of the music or the formality or informality of the service or the architecture of the building. It has to do with the nature of God. The only God worthy of worship is the One who knows the sufferings of his people (Exod. 3:7–8) and identifies with the hungry, the homeless, the imprisoned, the sick, the poor (Matt. 25). Only worship that celebrates God's presence with and love for the outcasts and leads to justice for them is really worship of God. Anything less is idol worship.

The preparation for and conduct of worship of God is taken entirely too lightly in our churches. A coordinated, coherent, theologically grounded order of service requires thorough preparation and sensitive leadership by pastors and laity. The reality of God known in the Exodus and supremely in Jesus Christ must be the central focus. Announcing the reign of God's kingdom of justice, compassion and joy is far more important than promoting an institution or satisfying people's narcissistic needs.

LET US PRAY!

A BISHOP IN THE KOREAN METHODIST CHURCH TOLD A recent gathering of Methodist bishops and presidents from around the world that the most often asked question by local churches of prospective pastors is this: "Is he/she a praying pastor?"

I don't recall that any Pastor-Parish Relations Committee has raised that question during my three years as a bishop in the United Methodist Church. Perhaps it is assumed that pastors are praying pastors; however, from the list of expectations and desired qualities given to the Cabinet, commitment to a life of prayer does not receive high priority. Pastors are expected to be inspiring preachers, diligent pastoral visitors, creative administrators, and personable community leaders. I have heard many evaluations of pastors; however, I know of no pastor who has been criticized for praying too much or too little.

Without a life of persistent cultivation of the presence of God and an attempt to discern the purposes of God, all other skills and qualities become superficial. The pastor is to be shaped by the nature and presence and purposes of God; otherwise, he/she functions primarily as a professional religionist or an institutional chief executive officer. Practicing the presence of God, therefore, must be a priority.

Prayer must be the priority of the congregation as well as the pastor. In most Methodist churches in Korea, laity participate in daily prayer meetings at the church early in the mornings. Prayer is central to their life as a community, not committee meetings and other "church" activities. During my visit in Seoul, I attended a prayer meeting along with about five hundred members of one congregation. Gathering for prayer before going to work is part of the routine of a large percentage of our Methodist sisters and brothers in Korea.

Wonder what would happen if prayer really became central to our pastors and churches in Memphis and Tennessee Conferences? Perhaps we need to spend less time in business meetings and more time in prayer meetings. Our preaching, visiting, administration, and community leadership as pastors would be deepened. The fellowship, commitment, and mission of the congregation would more nearly reflect the presence and purposes of God.

In all seriousness: Let us pray.

ECONOMISM—THE MODERN WORLD'S GOD

D R. JOHN COBB IS ONE OF UNITED METHODISM'S MOST
provocative theologians. He is now retired after a long career as a
teacher at the Claremont School of Religion. He has devoted his life to
interpreting the Christian gospel in the light of contemporary issues
and challenges.

In a lecture last fall at Vanderbilt , Dr. Cobb contended that the god
of the contemporary world is economism. Life evolves around and is
dominated by economic issues. Nations, communities, and individuals
are shaped primarily by financial issues and concerns. Our identity is
formed by the logic of the market place, and our worth is determined
by what we have to exchange in the consumerist economy.

Dr. Cobb contends that religion once shaped people's identity and
life. People identified themselves as Catholics, Protestants, Calvinists,
Anglicans, etc. Wars were fought over religious beliefs and people were
willing to defend their religion with their lives. The cruelty of the
Crusades began to diminish the influence of religion as the foundation
of life.

Religion gave way to nationalism as the formative shaper of life.
Being German, French, or English was more important than being
Catholic, Protestant, or Anglican. Wars were fought over national,
not religious, security and sovereignty. People identified themselves
primarily in terms of their nationality. Patriotism became the highest
expression of heroism. Dr. Cobb contends that nationalism began to
wane when the tragic events of Nazism became apparent to the
world.

Although vestiges of both religionism and nationalism continue,
Dr. Cobb contends that economism now dominates the world. Wars
are fought primarily over economic issues. Summits are now economic
summits. Finances are now the "bottom line." Almost everything is
controlled by profits, including scientific research, health care delivery,
food production and distribution, housing policy, and religious activity.
Personal worth and identity are measured in terms of "how much
he/she has." Reality is synonymous with economics. Being realistic
means being financially viable. Destructive and morally questionable

activities are now promoted in the name of income production. Gambling is the prime example.

The Bible challenges religionism, nationalism, and economism. Only the God revealed in the Exodus and in Jesus Christ is a worthy foundation for the shaping of life. Only God's vision of a healed creation, a world without religious, national, and economic barriers, and a humanity committed to justice and compassion is worthy of our final allegiance. God's kingdom transcends all religions, nations, and economic systems. May we be shaped by that kingdom!

EVERYBODY'S PRESENCE MATTERS

EMILY BRONTË, THE ENGLISH NOVELIST, WAS TAKEN BY HER clergyman father one spring morning to view the English moors. The fields were blanketed with the blooms of springtime flowers. The deadness of winter had been replaced with new life of spring. Emily's father wanted to impress his little eight-year-old daughter with the renewal of the earth by the presence of the warmth of the springtime sun.

He asked Emily, "What is here that was not here a hundred years ago?" She answered promptly, "Me."

The little girl's answer was unexpected, but it was a good response. Each person is a new factor in every situation, for good or ill, for blessing or cursing. Every person creates different dynamics simply by being present.

We have all experienced the power of an individual's presence. Groups change as persons enter them, or as persons leave them. Some groups become more loving, more joyful, more insightful because of the presence of one person. On the other hand, the whole atmosphere can disintegrate as the result of another's presence.

We underestimate the power of one person's presence, especially our own. "I'm only one person" is a favorite rationalization for passive acceptance of existing evil. Or, I have often heard persons excuse their absence from church with "The church is so big nobody will miss me."

Everybody's presence matters! Each person has resources needed to solve the problems that plague our world. Everyone can do something! The world is so interdependent that we are part of the answer or part of every problem confronting the world—poverty, crime, violence, racial hatred, injustice, drug and alcohol addiction, etc.

Since we are unique individuals with peculiar gifts, we bring something new to every situation. Our presence enriches or diminishes, blesses or curses, creates or destroys, builds up or tears down. God has chosen the human personality as a primary vehicle of the divine presence. Each person, then, has the potential of being a means of God's presence and action.

Your church needs your presence! You make a difference!

MORE THAN FORGIVENESS

I HEARD A SPEAKER AT A RECENT CONFERENCE ON evangelism say that the heart of the Christian gospel is the forgiveness of sins. He affirmed that the primary task of the evangelist is the proclamation that God forgives sin.

I would not reduce the importance of God's forgiveness. God's gracious acceptance of us in spite of our sin is good news. In Christ, God takes the initiative to justify and reconcile us. The Scriptures remind us that "God remembers our sin no more." It is a powerful truth: "If we confess our sin, God is faithful and just; He will forgive our sin and cleanse us from all unrighteousness."

God, however, does more with sin than forgive it. The total destruction of sin is God's goal. Jesus Christ did not die only to forgive us; Christ died to destroy the powers of sin and death. The gospel has more to do with the defeat of sin than with the removal of guilt feelings. Any evangelism that announces forgiveness without proclaiming God's intent on stopping our sin falls short of the full gospel.

John Wesley emphasized that God's grace includes sanctification and justification. We are not only saved from something; we are saved for something. God is not content to forgive us and leave us as we are. Grace transforms us into new creatures. According to Wesley, justification (forgiveness) is followed by a continuous process of being made perfect in love. Nothing less than holiness of heart and life, the total restoration of the divine image, is the goal.

God also incorporates us into a community of reconciled people who are called to be agents of reconciliation. Acceptance of God's forgiveness and destruction of sin carries with it a mission. The reconciled are to be agents of reconciliation. That is, God not only forgives our sin and enters the struggle to destroy it; God calls us to join the divine mission of defeating the powers of sin that threaten the world.

According to Wesley, God raised up the Methodists to "reform the nation, particularly the church, and to spread Scripture holiness throughout the land." God did not call us simply to forgive us. God can use us to announce the fullness of divine forgiving, sanctifying, and empowering grace.

Yes, God does more than forgive sin!

ON BEING AWARE OF THE TWILIGHT

WILLIAM O. DOUGLAS, LATE SUPREME COURT JUSTICE, cautioned a group of young lawyers in a letter, September 1976: "As nightfall does not come all at once, neither does oppression. In both instances, there is a twilight. . . . And it is in such twilight that we all must be aware of change in the air—however slight—lest we become unwitting victims of darkness."

Evil seldom comes like a thunderclap or a sudden eclipse of the sun. It most often arrives inconspicuously and gradually enfolds its victims. Evil's beginnings are usually hidden and unnoticed, frequently masquerading as harmless, or even as good. Only after it has erupted into personal or social tragedy is sin easily recognized.

The Nazi holocaust began long before the first Jews were rounded up and herded into gas ovens. It began in socially acceptable racial and religious prejudices. Because the masses, including the many religious leaders, were unaware of the twilight they became unwitting victims of darkness.

Slavery did not begin with the tearing of the first victims from their families and homeland and selling them as cattle. Slavery started with the notion that some persons are less-than-beloved children of God. That notion continues and often shows up as "harmless" jokes and politically acceptable segregation and discrimination. Oppression, like the night, does not come all at once.

It is twilight in this land. We are in danger of becoming unwitting victims of darkness! Evil is spreading its canopy wider, blocking the sunlight of justice, mercy, and compassion. In the name of welfare and medical reform, hostility toward the most defenseless children of God has become politically expedient. Under the guise of preventing crime and stopping violence, prisons are filling up and cries for the death penalty grow louder. Gambling, which insults the logic of grace and justice, has become a growth industry promoted by state and local governments.

The welfare system and medical care need reforming. Crime is a serious problem. Governments need money without placing undue burdens on their citizens. It isn't reform or the necessity of dealing with crime or efforts to provide fiscally sound governments that are the evidence of approaching oppression. It is the mean-spiritedness, the self-serving motivations, and the hostility toward those who "don't measure up."

The absence of compassion, magnanimity, and justice toward the most vulnerable people is a sure sign of approaching nightfall. Change is in the air. Twilight has arrived. Will we become unwitting victims of the darkness?

IT IS EASY TO BECOME WHAT WE HATE

THE SYNDICATED COLUMNIST, WILLIAM RASPBERRY, USED Mark Fuhrman as an example of the way evil evolves. Raspberry writes: "He [Fuhrman], to judge from the infamous tapes, hates it when people he 'knows' to be guilty are let go because of some technicality—a warrantless search, an unlawful seizure, insufficient evidence or some such. He has acknowledged . . . that he is not above making the evidence sufficient, by manufacturing it if necessary." He attempts to stop crime with criminal behavior. He counters dishonesty and cheating by becoming dishonest. He becomes what he hates.

Evil and good originate in the same Garden. Seldom does evil set out to be evil. It usually evolves from a desire to stop another's real or perceived evil. Hatred of evil is the birthplace of both saintliness and sinfulness. People often become monsters while destroying monsters, and the result is self-righteous monsters, the most dangerous kind.

The truth is, God is dishonored more by professed defenders than by identified enemies. Those who crucify Jesus usually do it in the name of resisting evil. Persecution of heretics is a greater evil than the heresy defended against.

It is tempting to fight evil with evil, violence with violence, anger with anger, hatred with hatred. The airwaves are full of appeals to do just that. The mean-spirited rhetoric of hatred and attack is heard from the religious/political right and the left. Both sides simply take on the character of what they dislike in the other.

God saw the evil of the world and sought to destroy it. Rather than taking on the character of the evil God hates, God battles evil with unquenchable love. Jesus Christ is God's ultimate response to evil. Even when evil nailed perfect goodness to a cross, Jesus responds with "Father, forgive them." He fought hatred with love, cruelty with acts of mercy, and violence with turning the other cheek.

We want to be good, honorable, and peaceable people. Goodness, integrity, justice, and peace are goals we seek. Never should we give up on the pursuit of such values. But we must beware of the tendency to use evil means to achieve good ends. The means used to defend against evil can make us evil. We so easily become what we hate. Paul stated it clearly: "Do not be overcome by evil, but overcome evil with good" (Rom. 12:21).

The power to follow Paul's admonition comes from the example and presence of the crucified and risen Christ.

"THANK YOU" ISN'T ALWAYS GRATITUDE

OUR GRANDDAUGHTER KATELYN IS BEGINNING TO TALK. One of the first phrases she learned was "Thank you." Linda and I had the privilege recently of taking care of Katelyn for a couple of days. Much to our amazement and pride she would respond to almost everything we did for her with a polite, "Thank you, Pawpaw," or "Thank you, Mawmaw." We are delighted that she is so polite at such an early age. Indeed gratitude is an appealing and needed virtue.

Katelyn's "Thank you, Pawpaw," did something to me. I wanted to do more for her. I found myself giving her more ice cream and playing one more game with her just so I could hear her say, "Thank you, Pawpaw." That could be dangerous for both Katelyn and me.

"Thank you" can be a form of manipulation. Katelyn could get the idea that expressing gratitude is just a way to get what she wants. It works better than crying and a temper tantrum. Of course, that would be but a polite form of selfishness, not gratitude.

My doing things for Katelyn just to be the recipient of her thanksgiving exposes my own selfishness. Doing good to another in order to be appreciated, admired, and thanked is less than mature love. It is a magnanimous expression of egotism, not authentic compassion.

Albert Schweitzer once wrote, "Take warning from the realization that thoughtless people generally complain most about ingratitude." Dr. Schweitzer's warning reverses conventional wisdom. We assume that thoughtlessness lies in those who fail to express gratitude. Schweitzer contends that thoughtless folks are the ones most conscious of ingratitude in others. He observed that concern for the ingratitude of the recipients of our benevolence exposes the superficiality of our motives. Rather than doing good for its own sake we use gratitude as "a lasso to bring others into our indebtedness."

Gratitude is fundamental to Christian discipleship. Genuine obedience grows out of gratitude for God's unmerited, undeserved love bestowed upon us without strings attached. Sharing in God's life and mission is our expression of gratitude, not a means of manipulating God to give us what we want.

Thanksgiving goes to the heart of life's meaning and purpose. Without authentic gratitude rooted in love, "Thank you" degenerates into polite manipulation and masked egotism. When motivated and shaped by love, "Thank you" strengthens relationships and multiplies compassion.

THE MOST NEGLECTED SPIRITUAL DISCIPLINE

R EADING THE BIBLE, PRAYING, ATTENDING PUBLIC WORSHIP, sharing in Holy Communion—these have been widely affirmed by Christians as vital spiritual disciplines. Neglect of them diminishes spiritual health, and most of us admit our lack of diligence in pursuing "holiness of heart and life" through such spiritual disciplines.

One discipline, however, rarely appears in the lists of required components of mature discipleship. It is, in my opinion, the most neglected act of devotion among United Methodists. In fact, few even consider it a necessary mark of spiritual health. Without it, however, the other disciplines lack power and authenticity.

The spiritual discipline most neglected by contemporary United Methodists is visitation of and friendship with the poor. Although the Bible clearly includes acts of mercy and justice toward the poor as indispensable components of authentic discipleship, most of us limit our relationships with the poor to occasional alms giving. Visiting "the widow and the orphan," ministry with "the least of these," and public policy decisions are left to agencies, hired employees, or elected representatives. Yet, we can no more delegate relationships with the poor to others than we can attain spiritual maturity by hiring another to read the Bible or pray or attend worship for us.

John Wesley clearly considered regular, ongoing relationships with the poor as indispensable for discipleship as the other disciplines. He required the early Methodists to not simply send their aid to the poor, but to take it to them.

Relationships with the poor are necessary because God is among them. Through them God comes to us! Wesley was convinced that grace most often comes not from the powerful to the weak but from the weak to the powerful. Otherwise, we would assume that salvation results from our own power and not from God's grace.

Although Bible reading, prayer, and attending the public ordinance of God are practiced too seldom, the most neglected spiritual discipline is visitation of the poor. And, we are spiritually impoverished thereby!

It's the Perspective That Counts

THERE USED TO BE A COVERED BRIDGE OVER TWELVE hundred feet long in New England. The story goes that a Yankee farmer who had never crossed it approached it with a wagon load of hay. After one look down that long, dark wooden tunnel, he turned his team of horses around and started in the other direction. Asked why he was turning around the farmer shrugged his shoulders and said, "Well, I could get in all right, but blamed if I could ever squeeze this load through that little hole on the other end!"

He was betrayed by his perspective. The light at the end of the tunnel was deceptively small. The intervening darkness obscured the breadth of the opening at the other end. The farmer's limited vision prevented him from reaching his destination.

In this age of demographic studies, sociological projections, strategic planning, and visioning processes, we don't enter the tunnels unless we are sure we can get out on the other side. We are hesitant to enter the tunnel unless the darkness has been removed and the exit on the other end measured. Most of us avoid the risks involved in pursuing worthy goals. Unless we are assured of success, we turn back toward the familiar and the manageable.

Sometimes the darkness of our personal lives overwhelms the light at the other end. Can we squeeze the load being carried through the other side? Withdrawing into a safe cocoon or turning toward the imagined security of an idealized past seems preferable to moving toward an uncharted future.

Faith is the willingness to enter the tunnel when the light at the other end seems small and obscure. The Hebrew slaves stepped into the raging sea with little assurance that the waters would part. They marched toward the Promised Land without a road map or advanced lodging reservations. The fishermen left their nets to follow the One who said, "'Follow me, and I will make you fish for people'" (Matt. 4:19). They knew little of what lay ahead for them or the One who called them.

Faith in the God revealed in Jesus Christ does not remove the tunnels and the darkness. It does, however, offer two promises: No one enters the tunnel alone, and the One present within the darkness is also the light at the other end. We follow One who has entered the tunnels and emerged triumphant!

FINDING OUR MORAL RUDDER

TOM BAXTER, CHIEF POLITICAL WRITER FOR THE *Atlanta Journal-Constitution*, wrote an article entitled "Susan Smith Case Echoes Bible Stories." It is a provocative and probing analysis of the Susan Smith saga. He writes:

> This column is usually about politics, but the Smith case has nothing to do with politics. It is about how iniquity, begun in the privacy of home, can bring calamity on an entire community. It is about how furtive actions can speak louder than words sung out in church, and about the terrible cost of lives lived with no moral rudder.
>
> The issues raised in this case weren't settled in the last election, nor will they be in the next one. They will only be put to rest on that day when all of us are judged, and the darkest secrets of our hearts revealed.

The loss of a moral rudder leads to calamity. Individuals, families, communities and nations suffer the consequences. The story of Susan Smith, who drowned her two little boys, exposed dark secrets of one small town; but, in a deeper sense, it also exposed the demonic forces present in all of us and in every community. Though we may not be tempted to kill our children, sexual misconduct and its subsequent secret-keeping and the refusal to respond to indications of abuse and neglect are akin to the demons which resulted in the horrible tragedy in Union, South Carolina.

Baxter is correct. The stories are as old as the Bible itself. The saints of the Old and New Testaments have clay feet. Sin is real and universal. None of us can, with innocence, point an accusing finger at another. The punishment of another's transgressions never absolves us of our own guilt and need for repentance.

The Bible also confronts us with the solution to our moral muddle. There we have a God revealed whose very character is love, justice, and righteousness. We are called to reflect God's character and nature in everything we are and do.

Furthermore, this God of righteousness, justice, and love holds us accountable. Our actions are judged. Evil has consequences. God forgives by entering into our struggles and temptations and by persistently holding before us what life is meant to be. Jesus Christ is the incarnation of God's dream for us all. God's revelation in Jesus Christ is our moral rudder.

THE RELIGIOUS IGNORANCE EXPLOSION

TODAY, KNOWLEDGE IN MANY AREAS IS EXPLODING. FOR example, the space it would take if all the information contained in one handful of earth were to be put in the *Encyclopedia Britannica* it would fill all fifteen volumes. Much of the biology taught in high school today was not even known when I was a student. Computers were mere speculations of a generation ago. Now the market life of a microprocessor before it is either copied or becomes obsolete averages only six to nine weeks. We are experiencing an information overload. We know more than we know what to do with what we know.

The knowledge explosion, however, is being accompanied by an ignorance explosion. We are becoming a society of specialists. Individuals know more and more about less and less. One simply cannot keep up with all the emerging information in his/her field of expertise, much less be well-informed on many subjects. Specialists have to immerse themselves in a limited area to remain competent and up-to-date.

The danger of specialization is the accompanying narrow perspective and the loss of the big picture. Medical specialists have trouble seeing and treating the whole person. Researchers can become so engrossed in following the information trail that they forget for what they are looking. The what and the how become more important than the why and the who. Meaning and purpose and values get pushed aside by preoccupation with the measurable, the marketable, the pragmatic, and the programmable. Literature, music, art, and religion are viewed as less important than science, technology, economics, business, and politics.

Religion has traditionally provided the broader perspective, the world view into which all categories fit. Theology, knowledge of God, was once considered to be the queen of the sciences. Now it isn't considered a science at all. Religion raises the questions of meaning, value, purpose. In theology, *why* is a more important question than *how* or *what*. Poetry and story, art and music are vehicles and avenues for the expression of the deeper kind of knowledge without which all other knowledge becomes blind at best and dangerous at worst.

The most educated today have little knowledge of religion. In fact, 60 percent of U.S. colleges do not offer any courses in religion. Ninety percent of college students take no religion course. Consequently, the subject about which the majority of the most educated in our society know the least is religion.

The growing religious ignorance represents a formidable challenge to the church and its colleges and universities. The situation calls for renewed support of church-related schools such as Lambuth University and Martin Methodist College, where religion is a vital part of the curriculum inside and outside the classroom.

GRATITUDE—MORE THAN
COUNTING BLESSINGS

A UTHENTIC GRATITUDE SELDOM COMES FROM COUNTING blessings. In fact, simply listing reasons to be thankful often results in arrogance and self-righteousness or discouragement and despair, depending on the length of the list.

History's most profound expressions of thanksgiving have emerged from circumstances in which there seemed to be few reasons to give thanks. Many psalms of thanksgiving date from national evil or personal suffering. On the night before he was betrayed and crucified, Jesus broke bread and gave thanks. Paul, who knew life's ups and downs, wrote "In all things give thanks." The hymn "Now Thank We All Our God" was written during the devastating Great Plague in Europe. The pilgrims, in the midst of deprivation, paused to give thanks. And, the proclamation declaring the first national day of thanksgiving was issued by President Lincoln during the carnage of the Civil War.

Giving thanks in all things requires a particular orientation toward life. Gratitude emerges from humble recognition that life is a gift to be celebrated, nurtured, and used for the enrichment of others. In every fiber of existence, we are dependent upon that which we do not create—from our biological nature to the environment which sustains us to persons and institutions which help shape us.

Genuine gratitude is a response to grace. Everything is a mysterious, gracious gift—the air we breathe, the food we eat, the love we share, the truth we perceive, the noble dreams we pursue. We are bound together in the profound mystery of life brought into being by God who loves us, redeems us, empowers us, and calls us toward a new heaven and a new earth.

Gratitude, too, is a gift from God. So we pray with one of our forbears, "O God, who has given me so much: Give me one thing more— a grateful heart."

CAN WE TALK ABOUT VALUES, MEANING, AND FAITH?

I T SEEMS TO BE INCREASINGLY DIFFICULT TO TALK meaningfully in our society about the essence of religion—values, meaning, and faith. Several factors account for the difficulty.

For one thing, we have lost our common story and language. It used to be that stories from the Bible and literature were part of our collective memories and vocabulary. References to Joseph and the Pharaoh, Moses and Miriam, Jacob and Esau, Deborah and David, the Good Samaritan and the Rich Young Ruler, the Prodigal Son and the Lost Sheep were easily recognized and understood. Stories which deal with meaning and morality were common reference points for discussion. That is no longer the case.

Furthermore, our society tends to be shaped more by science, technology, and economics than by art, poetry, and religion. The bottom lines are technological feasibility and financial profitability. Questions of transcendent meaning, inherent worth, and ethical value are pushed to the margins of public discussion. Does it work? Is it cost effective, marketable, and lucrative? Those are considered to be the relevant questions. What is its meaning? What does it say about the nature and purpose of life and God? Such questions seems irrelevant and merely speculative.

The difficulty in discussing values, meaning, and faith in the public arena was brought home to me in a recent forum on the patenting of genes. I participated in a widely publicized press conference along with representatives of the major religious groups in the United States. We attempted to raise the issue of the ethical and religious implications of patenting life forms and reducing them to their market value. It was difficult, if not impossible, for the media representatives to move beyond questions of the technical and scientific issues relative to genetics, the matter of the financing of research, and the necessity of making genetic science profitable. Many reports of the press conference trivialized the theological and ethical concerns and couched them in terms of science verses religion. They just didn't get it! Of course, some assumed that we didn't understand the technical/scientific and economic issues.

Politics is another reason for the difficulty in engaging in public discussion of values and religion. Many of the ethical and theological concerns have become so political that the exercise of power is more important than the discovery of the truth. The language and images of religion and values are used as rhetoric by which self-serving agendas are marketed to the public. Both inside and outside the church, the language of religion is used to garner political power. When power replaces the humble search for truth, dialogue ceases and the community becomes fragmented.

A major challenge confronting the church is the creation of communities in which honest discussion of values, meaning, and faith can take place. May our local churches be places where we can speak the truth in love (Eph. 4:15).

THE TOUGH MIND AND THE TENDER HEART

JESUS SENT HIS DISCIPLES INTO THE WORLD WITH THIS admonition: "'. . . be wise as serpents and innocent as doves'" (Matt. 10:16). He was affirming that effective and responsible discipleship calls for a tough mind and a sensitive heart. Either without the other is inadequate and dangerous.

The tough mind is important. Almost anything said about the importance of education is an understatement. Creative and productive living in the contemporary world requires a mind that can grapple reasonably, analytically, and with historical perspective.

However, education or reason alone fall short in meeting the most pressing problems in today's world. A tough mind can be demonically employed. History documents that knowledge can be but "improved means to unimproved ends."

Some of the most heinous crimes against humanity have been perpetrated by highly educated, knowledgeable people. Nazism, for example, took hold in a nation that was among the most educated in the world. C. S. Lewis stated it sharply when he said that knowledge without a proper sense of values creates but "clever devils." I suppose a clever devil is even more dangerous than an ignorant one.

A sensitive, compassionate heart is needed alongside a tough mind. But a sensitive heart without a tough mind is also inadequate, even dangerous. A tender heart undisciplined and unchecked by a perceptive mind falls prey to naive sentimentalism and offers superficial solutions to complex problems.

The church seeks to nurture both the tough mind and the tender heart. Through worship, Christian education, and loving relationships, the church feeds the mind with the truth of the faith and sensitizes the heart with the love of God. In so doing, the church helps persons be faithful disciples in a threatening and complex world.

The world desperately needs the witness of the tough-minded and the tenderhearted. Let us be "wise as serpents and harmless as doves."

JESUS IS REJECTED IN HIS HOMETOWN

ACCORDING TO LUKE, THE FIRST PEOPLE TO REJECT JESUS were his neighbors, those who had known him the longest. The occasion for their rejection was a worship service. His friends, maybe some relatives, and others who had known him all his life reacted violently when he read the scripture in his hometown Nazareth synagogue. After the service, they took him out of town and almost threw him off a cleft.

What accounts for the violent rejection of Jesus by his longtime neighbors and family friends in Nazareth? Since no explanation is given by the Gospel writer, we must look for the answer in the Scripture read, the context in which the passage was read, and Jesus' comments.

Jesus read from Isaiah 61: "'The spirit of the Lord is upon me, because he has anointed me to bring good news to the poor. He has sent me to proclaim release to the captives and recovery of sight to the blind, to let the oppressed go free, to proclaim the year of the Lord's favor'" (Luke 4:18–19).

The people who attended the synagogue in Nazareth that day had heard the passage on other occasions. No doubt many of them could recite it from memory. So, it wasn't the newness of the call to justice for the poor and oppressed that caused Jesus' longtime acquaintances to reject him.

Two things seemed to have upset them. One, Jesus said, "Today the Scripture is fulfilled in your hearing." The notion that God's action on behalf of the poor, the blind, the captives was taking place that day in and through one of their own threatened the status quo. Those who were benefitting from things as they were may have wanted the kingdom to come, but not yet. When God's reign comes to fruition, some folks will have to give up privilege, power, and prestige. The privileged, powerful, and prestigious prefer to keep the prophetic pronouncement as a future expectation rather than a present fulfillment.

I suspect, too, that Jesus' neighbors wanted special attention from the One whose reputation had already grown in Capernaum, the home of many foreigners and non-Jews. Maybe they were upset because their hometown celebrity didn't limit his miracles to hometown folks. It is always upsetting when that which we want is given to another.

For whatever reason, the people who knew Jesus the longest rejected him first. The church has known Jesus for two thousand years. He has been the subject of our hymns, sermons, and Bible studies for twenty centuries. Yet, the contemporary church often keeps its distance from the poor, and reflects society's racism, sexism and classism, and it is often captive to privilege and prestige.

Could it still be true? Is Jesus still rejected in his own home, the church?

WE NEED BOUQUETS AND CABBAGES

I RAN ACROSS THIS STATEMENT RECENTLY: "EVERY HOME needs a bouquet as surely as it needs a cabbage." It was the author's way of saying that beauty is as important as food.

It reminded me of an incident recorded in the New Testament (Matt. 26:6–13, Mark 14:3–9, John 12:1–8). A woman broke an elegant vase and used its expensive contents to anoint Jesus. The disciples, led by Judas, protested the act as a useless waste of money. After all, the vase and ointment could have been sold and the money used to feed the poor.

Jesus, however, challenged the disciples to consider another meaning of the woman's act. They reduced her act of devotion to its economic value. Jesus affirmed, "She has done a beautiful thing." He went on to suggest that her unselfish, lavish expression of devotion was also a symbol that pointed beyond monetary matters.

We are becoming increasingly utilitarian in our approach to life. the principal criteria of evaluation is cost and utility. Such a world has little place for bouquets, only cabbages.

In a utilitarian world, education is reduced to a means of increasing earning power rather than a search for truth and wisdom. Careers are chosen according to the salary available rather than the opportunities for service afforded. Music, art, literature, and even worship become slaves of the market place. Will it sell? That often becomes the only deciding director. The ability to lift the spirit, inspire noble living, and cleanse the soul seldom enters the equation.

What if God had decided to limit creation to what sells or to what has mere utilitarian value? There would be no multi-colored landscapes or blooming rose gardens to decorate the earth. There would be no music sung by chanting birds or flowing fountains or played as symphonies. Art and literature and even worship would not be.

But the fact is, we humans need beauty expressed in art and music and poetry and nature as certainly as we need bread and oxygen. We need symbols as surely as we need sunshine.

God is beauty, truth, goodness, love. To be insensitive to beauty, unappreciative of truth, blind to goodness, and calloused to love is to miss God. On the other hand, to cultivate an awareness of beauty, to be committed to truth, to strive for goodness, and to grow in love is to know God.

Worship is a means of countering utilitarianism. Worship is never self-serving. It is an expression of adoration of God. Worship can sensitize us to goodness and surround us with love. When it does, it is "a beautiful thing" which transcends economics and pragmatics.

CHRISTIANS HAVE PROBLEMS TOO

I HEARD A PREACHER SAY RECENTLY, "IF YOU ACCEPT CHRIST you can say goodbye to those inner conflicts, depression, and problems. Christ is the answer to all that ails you."

Such a superficial generalization is misleading in its assessment of the human struggle and in its interpretation of the Christian faith. In this narcissistic age, however, such a promise has appeal. It is the same appeal offered by drugs, alcohol, pop psychology, and segments of the commercial world. The right chemical, or proper mental attitude, or an available product will set you free from such nagging human problems as guilt, grief, depression, interpersonal conflict, anger, frustration, inferiority, and insecurity.

We have gotten the notion that to be mature and Christian means to rise above such maladies. One result of such an assumption is denial of problems, which leads to repression, escapism and other unhealthy defense mechanisms. Another possible result is despair and disillusionment, for eventually, the inadequacy of the offered solution surfaces.

The essence of the gospel lies elsewhere. The good news of God's unconditional love enables us to face our problems and weaknesses, knowing we are accepted and valued. Accepting God's grace doesn't magically remove us from the inevitable struggles of the human predicament. It does provide a context in which to face and endure the struggles. Furthermore, accepting Christ provides a direction toward which to move.

Christians have problems too. But they also know that they are accepted and loved in the midst of the problems and that there is hope for weaving even the maladies into the fabric of wholeness.

Accepting Christ may create some inner conflicts and struggles as surely as provide solace and comfort. Christ is the Great Disturber as well as the Comforter. Accepting one without the other perverts the faith and distorts human personality.

SIN IS TO BE FORGIVEN, NOT FORGOTTEN

RECOVERING INNOCENCE IS A POWERFUL HUMAN DRIVE. We will do almost anything to escape guilt. We desperately try to forget our sin. Alcohol, drugs, busyness and even religion are readily available means of numbing our memories.

History is often recorded and remembered in such a way as to omit our collective sin. Wars are chronicled as political and national victories or defeats rather than personal, family and community destroyers. The history books I read in school described the European expansion into the Americas as discovery and quest for freedom and glossed over the genocide visited on native peoples and the cruel enslavement of Africans. There are some today who would have us believe that the holocaust never happened. Our recollections of the past seem to contain more boasting than confession.

In fact, confession is all but vanishing, even from our services of worship. In an age of positive thinking, "feel good" religion, and entertainment disguised as worship, remembering sin and repenting have fewer and fewer practitioners. Grace is being cheapened to mean being saved without being changed. Forgiveness is being reduced to a casual, "Ah, forget it."

God's forgiveness may permit God "to remember our sin no more," but we had better not forget them. Forgotten sins are repeated sins. Forgiveness without repentance made real by remembrance leaves us unchanged. Contemporary events provide ample evidence that attempts to forget sin only multiply it. Sin buried alive in the memory surfaces on new occasions and often in ever more destructive ways.

Forgiveness is infinitely more than forgetting. It is remembering our sin before God. Forgiveness means reconciliation and a new beginning made possible by God's grace, not by our forgetfulness. God's grace makes possible the remembrance of our sin in the light of God's power to reconcile and change us. Because we are forgiven, we can remember our sin, repent, and be transformed.

If we do not remember and repent, we will forget and repeat. Let us confess our sins before God who forgives and changes us.

LET US CONFESS OUR SINS

A SUNDAY SCHOOL CLASS ONCE REQUESTED THE removal of the Prayer of Confession from the Sunday order of worship. I requested an opportunity to visit the class and discuss the matter.

Upon being asked the reasons for the request, the following were given:

- the Prayer of Confession reinforces a negative self-image Confession implies that we are bad people
- we aren't always guilty of the specific sins named in the Confession
- our children get a negative view of themselves
- we need to think positively and guilt is psychologically damaging
- worship should always be uplifting and ought to make us feel good

"The reasons given for removing the Prayer of Confession are among the reasons for including it," I replied. The refusal to acknowledge that we are sinners is the clear evidence of the presence of sin. Failure to repent and confess only covers the deadly presence of evil within us.

The contemporary emphasis on the cultivation of a positive self-image through positive thinking contradicts authentic theology and sound psychology. And, the notion that sin can be removed by ignoring it or attributing it to others only compounds its destructiveness. One pundit may have been right when he said that "original sin" is the only Christian doctrine that is empirically verifiable.

Sin is for real, and it is too serious to ignore. The Cross of Christ is the revelation of how serious sin is. It seeks to destroy God! It threatens everything God desires for humanity. Sin, not confession, is the real enemy of health and wholeness.

The Cross also reveals the solution to sin: God's costly forgiveness and reconciliation. The failure to face and confess our sin before God and one another exposes our weak faith in God's grace. It is not our positive thinking which removes our guilt; it is God's redemptive action. Let us confess our sin before God and one another.

WINNING IS HELPING OTHERS TO FINISH

IN A WONDERFUL SERMON AT A MEETING OF THE COUNCIL of Bishops, Jack Meadors, bishop of Mississippi, shared a powerful story which the whole church needs to hear.

During a Special Olympics, nine children lined up for the hundred-yard dash. The signal was given and the specially challenged children left the starting line. Several yards into the race, one contestant fell. He began to cry as he held his skinned knee. The other children heard the cry. All eight of them turned back toward their fellow runner. A girl with Down's syndrome knelt down and kissed the scratched knee of her friend. The other children lifted their competitor to his feet. Arm in arm they all walked across the finish line at the same time. Parents, coaches, friends, and members of the press rose to their feet and cheered the nine winners.

At least for a brief moment, those children provided a glimpse of the world as God intends it to be. They challenged the prevailing notion that winning means finishing first. They knew that ranking and ribbons and medals mean nothing. What matters is this: helping one another to join in and finish the race.

In the marketplace, on the playing field, and in the political arena, competition is touted as the indisputable law of life and the only sure way to success. Defeating, even destroying, one's competitors becomes the goal.

In the kingdom of God, however, cooperation is the sign of success. According to the One who incarnated the reign of God, Jesus Christ, the last shall be first and the greatest are the servants. Judgment is pronounced in accordance with what is done unto "the least of these." The willingness to lose everything for the sake of God's kingdom characterizes the true winners.

It doesn't really matter where we finish in the race, or how we rank in accordance with others. Winning is joining arms with others and pursuing the goal together, knowing that we are all supported by the Everlasting Arms.

What Is Success?

SEVERAL YEARS AGO A PARISHIONER GAVE ME A SUBSCRIPTION to a magazine entitled *Success Unlimited.* Each issue contained tips on how to succeed in business or athletics or politics. Numerous "success" stories were told as sources of inspiration and motivation.

Although the magazine editors never stated it explicitly, it was obvious that success was synonymous with wealth, winning, and prestige. Poverty, losing, and anonymity were treated as if they were social diseases or unpardonable sins. I am not sure the magazine continues, but the god of success by means of wealth and prominence and winning is very much alive.

Maybe the desire to succeed deserves nurturing. However, a new definition of success is required. The image we have of what it means to succeed is as determinative as the strength of our motivation to achieve it.

What does it mean to be successful? The question was asked Dr. Harry Emerson Fosdick toward the end of his long, creative life. What would you add to Dr. Fosdick's list?

- to laugh often and much
- to win respect of intelligent people and the affection of children
- to earn the appreciation of honest critics and endure the betrayal of false friends
- to appreciate beauty
- to find the best in others
- to leave the world a bit better, whether by a healthy child, a garden patch, or a redeemed social condition
- to know even one life has breathed easier because you lived

Success has more to do with what we are than what we have. It is measured more by how we serve than how we are served. It is determined more by what we enable others to be than what others enable us to achieve. Success has more to do with the power of love than it has to do with the love of power.

Jesus, the most successful person in human history, would never have appeared in a first-century edition of *Success Unlimited.*

A God Who Is Steadfast

A FARMER PUT A WEATHER VANE ON HIS BARN ON WHICH were inscribed the words "God is love." A neighbor said that he assumed it meant that if the wind blew in the right direction, God is love. "No," replied the farmer, "it means that no matter which way the wind blows, God is love."

The Bible testified to the relentless love of God. A favorite description of God in the Hebrew Scriptures is "steadfast love"—a steady, persistent love that will not let go. The faithfulness of God contrasts with human fickleness and betrayal. Although the people rebel and turn away from their divinely given purposes, God remains steadfastly faithful.

Jesus portrays God's faithfulness in the New Testament. ". . . he stedfastly set his face to go to Jerusalem," wrote Luke (9:51 KJV). Before him loomed the Cross, but he held firmly to his course. In the Garden of Gethsemane, he struggles with his destiny, but he remained steadfast. On the cross he cried, "My God, my God, why have you forsaken me?" But he remained faithful and finally declared, "It is finished."

Remaining steadfast, faithful, and loyal to the highest and best requires more than grit and determination. It requires a purpose big enough to withstand lesser callings and attractive distractions. And, it demands an awareness that we are not alone.

Faithfulness to Christlikeness is far from easy in a world dominated by consumerism, individualism, narcissism, hatred and violence. Steadfast love which reaches out to even "the enemy" is unnatural in a society that defines toughness as vengeance. Seeking the well-being of the community above one's own self-interest is viewed as weakness in a world where finishing first is everything.

The Cross reveals Christ's steadfastness in the pursuit of God's purposes. There he refused to be distracted from his purpose by the violence, hatred, misunderstanding, and betrayal of others. He prayed for their forgiveness and commended his own life into God's care. Imitating such steadfast love is a large enough purpose to demand our all.

The Cross also assures us that we aren't alone in our own struggles to be steadfast and faithful. The One who calls us to faithfulness will be with us even to the close of the age.

Goodness Goes Beyond Mere Obedience

THE LATE LORD MOULTON MANY YEARS AGO ISSUED AN appeal to the English people that they not limit their goodness to obedience of the law. He said: "The greatness of a nation lies in the number of its citizens who can be trusted to obey self-imposed law."

Almost every behavior we oppose results in efforts to pass a law. Legislation is a popular means of promoting goodness. Legislatures and law-enforcement personnel are expected to make us good. Current calls for more laws and more police officers are understandable pleas for solutions to problems of corruption, violence, and injustice.

Indeed, laws are necessary for an orderly society. Martin Luther King once said that civil rights' laws would not make white people love him, but legislation would keep the racist's foot off his neck.

Laws and their enforcement, however, are restraints on our badness more than reflections of our goodness. Jesus reminds us in the Sermon on the Mount that authentic goodness exceeds mere obedience to external laws. Restrained badness is not synonymous with goodness.

Genuine goodness comes from inner obligation which precedes and exceeds outer behavior. The Cross of Christ reflects a character that is obedient to the unenforceable obligation. Jesus voluntarily took upon himself what no one possibly could have demanded. He willingly gave his life for a higher purpose.

The essence of Christian living lies in rising above legalism and being and doing far more than any law can exact or any person require. This is the essence of Jesus' spirit and teaching. Turning the other cheek and going the second mile is the excess and extra gift of an inner obligation.

Mark Twain, at age sixty, committed himself to paying debts for which he had no legal obligation. He did so because, as he said, "Honor is a harder master than the law."

Obedience to the law is important. However, genuine goodness exceeds obedience. It consists of doing what is right even when there are no observable rewards or punishment. Goodness which "exceeds that of the Scribes and Pharisees" grows from inner transformation of the heart.

PIOUS PROFANITY

I HAVE A GOOD FRIEND WHO SERVED AS A CHAPLAIN IN A hospital for critically ill children. He shared with me an incident which raises serious questions in my mind about an all-too-popular notion about God and prayer.

My friend overheard a group of hospital volunteers complaining about the difficulty of finding a parking place. One volunteer, who drives into town on her assigned day, said, "Oh, I never have any trouble finding a parking place. I just pray and God always arranges a place for me."

I can't avoid asking, "If God is arranging parking spaces for wealthy suburbanites, why isn't God healing those critically ill kids whose parents are praying desperately for a miracle?" What kind of God would respond positively to a request for a convenient parking slot but seemingly turn deaf ears to a plea for the healing of a sick child? And if the woman has such effectiveness with prayer, why doesn't she use her influence with the Almighty on behalf of those children instead of her own convenience?

Athletes and other contestants often attribute their winning to God. Is God a partisan sports fan? Does God judge beauty contestants and pick the winner? Is God arranging the outcome of recreational events while wars rage, flood waters destroy cities, millions of children die of starvation, and people die prematurely by the thousands from ravaging diseases?

Reducing God to a personal convenience and prayer as a means to selfish ends is a deadly form of idolatry and blasphemy. It trivializes God and becomes a pious profanity. On the surface, it may appear to put God at the center of everything. But in reality, our wishes and desires are at the center. Prayer becomes a manipulative attempt to use God to accomplish our purposes.

God cannot be domesticated and put on a leash. Neither is prayer a means of coercing the Divine to fulfill our wishes. God is the Holy Other who transcends and judges all human desires, yet who is lovingly present within human struggles for wholeness, peace, justice, and righteousness. The appropriate responses to the Holy One are awe, reverence, and joyful commitment to God's purposes for all creation.

WE NEED TO TALK TO, NOT ABOUT

DIFFERENCES AND DISAGREEMENTS HAVE ALWAYS EXISTED in the church. Diversity of perspectives and beliefs can even be healthy and means of growth. One church member told me several years ago, "If you and I always agree, one of us is unnecessary."

Most of us, however, are uneasy with disagreements and controversies. Our uneasiness frequently takes the form of talking about those with whom we differ rather than talking to and with them. Consequently, battle lines get drawn and issues go unresolved.

More destructive than the current controversies existing within the United Methodist Church is the failure by competing voices to talk to one another. Like-minded folks get together to talk about and label those unlike them. They thereby reinforce their prejudices and justify their rejection of others. It is a devilish temptation to which we all succumb.

We can learn a valuable lesson from two giants of the early church. Peter and Paul had strong disagreements over a basic theological question: Do disciples of Jesus Christ have to be Jews first? Is circumcision required? Paul writes, "But when Cephas came to Antioch, I opposed him to his face . . ." (Gal. 2:11).

Paul went directly to Peter. He didn't form a caucus group to talk about Peter or to strategize how to counter his influence. Nor did he substitute a position paper or sermon for a personal encounter. Paul and Peter struggled together for insight into the mind and will of God.

Civil and constructive theological discussion is increasingly difficult in the contemporary church. Theology and doctrine have become politicized, and discourse is being replaced by power plays and intimidation strategies. The results include a distorted gospel, a fragmented community, and a lost mission.

Let us talk to and with those with whom we differ. In so doing, we may hear the voice of God.

TEMPTATIONS OF SUCCESS

A ARON STERN MAKES THIS TROUBLING ASSERTION IN HIS book *Me, The Narcissistic American*: "No society has ever survived success." Stern contends that success spawns narcissism—preoccupation with self—and narcissism spells destruction.

Many societies have survived war, disease, famine, and natural disaster. Hardship and struggle often challenge and call forth the best in individuals and societies. Once the hardships have been overcome and the struggles have ended, danger lurks in the shadows of the triumph.

Some of history's greatest failures have come on the heels of a victory. Immediately after winning the battle against the prophets of Baal, Elijah went into a dungeon of despair and cried, "O Lord, take away my life." In a matter of hours after he declared his unending loyalty to Jesus, Peter did what he said he would never do—he denied the One he loved! Little wonder that Paul warned, "Let any who think that they stand, take heed lest they fall."

Success often sows the seeds of future failure. Why? Why is it hard to survive success? For one thing, success encourages complacency. We assume that one victory insures persistent conquest. When it comes to the human spirit, however, the battle never ends. Evil is never totally defeated and daily vigilance is required.

Also, success tends to result in arrogance. Whereas acknowledged need leads to humble acceptance of aid, assumed success acknowledges no need of grace. No one is more vulnerable than the one who acknowledges no weakness.

Success often distorts priorities and blinds us to the values that matter most. Material prosperity, personal pleasure, and social prominence tend to become more important than generosity, sacrificial service, and personal integrity.

God's grace meets us in both defeat and victory. May the divine grace give us triumph over the temptations of failure and success.

THE ENTRENCHED MIND

I FIRST HEARD THE PHRASE ON A NATIONAL PUBLIC RADIO broadcast. An author, whose name I did not hear, referred to "the entrenched mind." She used the phrase to describe persons who spend so much time and energy defending their entrenched position that they have no openness to new insights and revelations. They never get out of their mental bunkers to explore a broader perspective.

It reminded me of the man's prayerful response upon hearing about evolution. He prayed, "O God, don't let it be true; but if it is true, don't let anybody hear about it."

I suppose we all suffer from "the entrenched mind." Bunkers protect the vulnerable. The more insecure we are, the more we fortify our positions against ideas which run counter to our own. Exposing our positions to the onslaught of diverse views risks having them shot down. It might lead to changing our position, which is an admission that we were wrong.

Bullying, intimidation, dogmatism, personal attacks, labeling, prooftexting—these are all weapons of the "entrenched mind." Insults, half-truths, innuendos, impugning of motives are the artillery shells lobbed from the mental bunkers of those who would rather defeat than understand.

Paul wrote, "Have this mind among yourselves, which you have in Christ Jesus . . ." (Phil. 2:5 RSV). The Christlike mind challenges the entrenched mind. According to Paul, the Christlike mind is characterized by humility, openness to God, and sacrificial service to humanity.

The Christlike mind comes out of the bunker and gives itself in love to God and others.

After all, the world needs more people who live God's truth and love than it needs those who simply defend their version of truth.

WHO ARE THE WINNERS?

ALMOST EVERYBODY WANTS TO BE A WINNER. FINISHING first, winning, conquering, and succeeding are popular goals, whether it be in sports, politics, professional pursuits, academics, or games. Aggressiveness, competitiveness, ranking, and achieving become prime values in a society that insists on having winners. Trophies, applause, league standings, recognition, honors, and publicity are viewed as outward and visible signs of inner success and superiority.

Though winning has its place, it can be a destructive illusion. Who are the winners? What is success? Spencer Haywood, a former professional basketball player, raised questions about the widely accepted image of a winner. He said in an interview, "They call me a superstar. I'll tell you who a superstar is. It's a guy raising six kids on $150 a week."

Jesus talked about winners. He contended that a winner is a despised Samaritan who stopped to help a wounded man along the road. A winner is a poor widow who out of sheer gratitude dropped her small coin in the collection box. A winner is a rejected tax collector who beat his breast in repentance saying, "God be merciful to me, a sinner." A winner is a woman from the street who anointed the Messiah's feet with precious oil in an act of devotion. Jesus declared that a winner is one who gives a drink to the thirsty, food to the hungry, clothing to the naked, one who visits the imprisoned, the sick, the lonely.

Jesus also described some losers. One was a Rich Young Ruler. He had three prized trophies—wealth, youthfulness, and power. But he was so tied to his wealth and power that he couldn't love. He was a loser. Another was a publicly acclaimed religious leader who thought he had won and thanked God that he was above such losers as extortioners, adulterers, and tax collectors. Another was a rich man who enjoyed the luxury of his great banquets and paid no attention to that "loser" Lazarus who sat at the gate begging for food. Or those prominent folks who pushed for the chief seats—they were losers.

The real winners are the servants of humanity. Winning means loving, cooperating, maintaining integrity. History's supreme winner is Jesus of Nazareth. Measured by contemporary standards, however, he was a loser. He was executed at a young age. He died alone, penniless. There was little evidence that his efforts had succeeded. But he won! He won the ultimate victory—a victory of love over hate, hope over despair, goodness over evil, justice over corruption. In the final analysis, that is the only kind of victory that really matters.

Two Kinds of Hypocrisy

A FRIEND WHO DOESN'T PARTICIPATE IN ANY CHURCH confronted me with a familiar charge, "The church is hypocritical." I have heard the charge many times, but this time it was different. Most persons who make such accusations seem to do so in a spirit of arrogance and self-righteousness as if to say, "At least I'm better than those hypocrites who go to church."

But this young man wasn't arrogant. His tone was one of regret and disappointment. I know that he is an honorable, compassionate man who exhibits many Christlike qualities. He seems to want to believe and would like to be proven wrong in his judgment upon the church.

However, who can deny that the church is hypocritical? If hypocrisy is the name given to the disparity between beliefs and practice, between affirmation and behavior, then the church may be more guilty than any other institution. No other institution has such high ideals or aspires to be more than does the church. Indeed, those whose practice and behavior totally reflect their beliefs and ideals have inadequate beliefs and ideals.

The church is a pilgrim people who have caught a glimpse of a new world, the kingdom of God. They are a people on their way to the Promised Land where the will of God is completely known and perfectly fulfilled. They have not yet arrived. Therefore, their reach exceeds their grasp; their deeds and dreams are not yet one and the same.

My young friend reminded me of another form of hypocrisy—those who practice more than they profess. That young man's failure to identify with the church may also be a form of hypocrisy. I know that he has incorporated in his life many of the goals and values affirmed by the church. He has experienced the realities of grace and forgiveness and he is committed to justice, goodness, and compassion. Yet, he has chosen not to identify himself with that community that has as its basic purpose and goal the incarnation of the kingdom of God. How unfortunate for him and the church.

Yes, there are hypocrites in the church who profess more than they yet practice, and there are hypocrites outside the church who may practice more than they yet profess. Both kinds of hypocrites need each other and we all need a double measure of the grace of God.

GOD CHOOSES DREAMERS

WHAT TRAIT CHARACTERIZES PERSONS AND GROUPS through whom God lifts the world closer to the divine purpose for it? Certainly morality and integrity are critically important. Clarity of belief about God is also a highly desirable quality of those who would be used by God. However, neither morality nor correct theological formulations seem to be the dominant traits of those whom God finds most ready to be instruments of transformation.

Look at the heroes of the faith. Abraham was willing to permit the Pharaoh to abuse Sarah if it would save his skin. Jacob cheated his brother out of the birthright and blessing. Moses was guilty of murder and attempted cover-up. Joseph was spoiled and insensitive as a youngster. David's tragic immorality is well-known. Jesus' disciples reflected human failures, confusion, and betrayal. Paul had a guilt-laden past, as did most of those whom we call "saints."

One common quality which enabled God to use Abraham, Jacob, Joseph, Moses, David, the disciples, Paul, and countless others is this: they were dreamers. They were captured by a vision of something God was doing or going to do. They got a glimpse of a new world and began to move toward it.

We are shaped as much by our vision of what ought to be as we are molded by our memory of what has been. Faith involves openness to the new world God is forever bringing and the willingness to live now in terms of that new world.

Walter Brueggeman describes the church as people who live toward a vision—God's vision. The world desperately needs special dreamers, those who dream God's dreams and give themselves to fulfilling them.

LEVELS OF LOVE

F REDERICK BEUCHNER DESCRIBES FOUR LEVELS OF LOVE IN *The Magnificent Defeat*. The first is love for equals—of friend for friend, sibling for sibling, spouse for spouse. It is love for that which is loving and lovely. Such love was characterized by Jesus as "loving those who love you." The world smiles at such love.

The second level is the love for the less fortunate—the love for those who suffer, those who are poor, those who are failures. Beuchner calls this compassion, and it touches the heart of the world.

The third level or form of love is rare. It is love for those who are more fortunate—those who succeed where we fail, those who have what we want. It is to rejoice without envy of those who rejoice. It is the love of the poor for the rich, the "D" and "F" student for those who make "As" and "Bs," the employee for the employer, the obscure for the prominent. The world is usually bewildered by such love.

Then there is the love for the enemy—the love for the one who does not love you but mocks, threatens, and inflicts pain. It is the tortured's love for the torturer, the oppressed for the oppressor, the victim for the criminal, the condemned for the executioner. This is God's love, according to Beuchner, and it is the love which conquers the world.

Love at each level is a gift which must be nurtured, cultivated, and shared. John Wesley understood holiness and Christian perfection as "being made perfect in love." Beuchner's four levels of love may help us identify where we are in our journey toward holiness or perfection. Maturing and reaching new levels of love involves accepting more fully God's love which reaches us wherever we are on the journey toward "being made perfect in love."

HAPPINESS IS A FALSE GOD

HAPPINESS HAS BECOME A POPULAR IDOL; IT IS A GOD THAT receives considerable time, money, energy, commitment and loyalty. "It makes me happy" has become the ultimate rationale for behavior.

The widespread assumption is that happiness consists of feeling comfortable, being turned on, having all appetites satisfied. It is the absence of pain, struggle, hardship. "If it feels good, do it" is the creed of the adherents of the happiness cult.

The cult is as old as it is pagan. The happiness god is one of the true God's oldest and most formidable rivals. Hedonism is one of its ancient philosophical names. Hedonism is the notion that the chief end of life is pleasure.

Not all hedonism is rooted in sensuous pleasure. The Epicureans, for example, believed that the highest pleasures are mental and aesthetic. Nevertheless, if we assume that pleasure, fun, comfort, and feeling good are life's supreme values, we are hedonists.

The bad thing about idols is their distortion of reality. Happiness as an idol results in the perversion of life and the destruction of persons. When happiness is made the chief god, unhappiness usually results.

The inescapable truth is that avoidance of pain, struggle, work, discipline and sacrifice also means the end of growth, intelligence, patience, courage, integrity, creativity, and love. Real living requires a lot of blood, sweat, and tears!

Jesus challenged the whole cult by transforming the meaning of happiness. He defined happiness as meekness, mercy, hunger, poverty, mourning, purity, peacemaking, and being persecuted for righteousness' sake. He said that life is to be found by losing it, in taking up a cross, in serving others, in giving away possessions, in being least.

Jesus, who is history's supremely happy person, knew what we haven't yet learned—happiness is the by-product of a committed life. It is a serendipity. The truly happy are those who so lose themselves in love for God and neighbor that they have no need to evaluate their own happiness.

LET US TEST THE SPIRITS

S OME OF THE MOST HEINOUS CRIMES AGAINST HUMANITY are committed in the name of religion. Nations and individuals have committed every form of brutality imaginable in the name of religious devotion. Adolf Hitler justified the extermination of six million people this way: ". . . I believe that I am acting in accordance with the will of the Almighty Creator; by defending myself against the Jew, I am fighting for the work of the Lord." Similar cruelty and inhumanity continue to be motivated by religion.

A German psychiatrist and Lutheran pastor, with whom I had the privilege of studying some thirty years ago, estimated that 40 percent of the emotionally ill persons who entered his Berlin clinic were suffering from maladjustments rooted in "sick religion." He warned: "A perverted understanding of the Christian faith kills thousands of people every year." He wrote a book entitled *Ecclessiogenic Neurosis*, neurosis induced by the church.

An age in which religion accounts for or contributes to many personal and social problems would do well to heed the admonition of the Epistle of John: ". . . do not believe every spirit, but test the spirits to see whether they are from God" (1 John 4:1).

Yet, many persons resist evaluating religion. They assume that any religious orientation is valid as long as the believers are sincere, or if it has a "Christian" label on it. The Bible and church history, however, document that the major theological conflicts are not between religion and non-religion or theism versus atheism. The destructive conflicts are between religion that liberates, sets free, and loves and religion that oppresses, enslaves and instills hate.

The writer of the Epistle of John reminds us that Jesus Christ, who is the embodiment of God's love, is the real test. He writes: ". . . he who loves is born of God and knows God. He who does not love does not know God; for God is love" (1 John 4:7–8 RSV).

GRATITUDE SPRINGS FROM GRACE

G RATITUDE ORIGINATES IN THE AWARENESS THAT WE ARE receivers and distributors more than we are creators and owners. The notion that anyone is "self-made" or that we "get what we deserve" typically results in arrogance and selfishness. Humility and gratitude, on the other hand, emerge from the realization that no one is self-made and that we get more than we deserve.

No one can honestly claim to be self-made. At best, we only develop and utilize the gifts received from multitudes of people. Who can claim to be self-created? Our bodies and minds are the product of millions of years of genetic "wheeling and dealing." We didn't create the land on which we live nor the institutions which feed us, govern us, educate us, medicate us, entertain us, and inspire us.

Conveniences we enjoy are the result of scientific and technological advances of countless inventors, researchers, engineers, technicians, artisans, and laborers. The food we eat comes from the fertile soil and seeds planted by numerous farmers, harvested by anonymous laborers, processed and transported by unknown workers, and marketed by numerous merchants.

Everywhere we turn we run into a gift; and every gift, when traced far enough, cost someone or someones their very lives. Follow the footprints of any gift and eventually the tracks are stained with blood.

Paul Tournier was right when he declared: ". . . there comes a day when a [person] understands that all is of grace, that the whole world is a gift from God, a completely generous gift. . . . We see each flower, each drop of water, each minute of our life as a gift of God."

Gratitude springs from the awareness that life is grace, a completely undeserved gift. The only appropriate expression of gratitude for grace is joyful sharing of the gifts received. Because we so freely receive, we so freely give.

FAITH IS MORE THAN POSITIVE THINKING

A MAN SAID TO HIS PASTOR: "I GO TO CHURCH TO BE MADE to feel better. I want to hear sermons about the birds singing, the sun shining, and the flowers blooming. I don't want to hear about any problems. Religion is supposed to make us feel better and more hopeful. We need to think positively!"

Faith is more than wishful thinking, the ability to smile pleasantly while others are in tears and wringing their hands. Some people have the impression that to have negative feelings, to hurt, to struggle, to get discouraged, is the absence of faith. Even in the midst of wrenching grief and throbbing pain we are told to "think positively," "look at the bright side," and "praise the Lord."

There is a grain of truth in the advice that we are to think positively. We must have hope in order to survive. Getting our thinking straight is part of the answer to many of our problems. How we think and feel about what happens is as determinative as the event itself. Our attitude does make a difference.

However, the positive-thinking approach is fraught with flaws and dangers. For one thing, it may become a form of denial and repression. To think positively and smile sweetly while our lives are being mangled or while the world unravels is a malignant form of escapism. Such self-deception gives free rein to the destructive forces that threaten us from within and without. Positive thinking is a placebo rather than a cure.

Superficial positive thinking may also contribute to our becoming unreal, pretentious people. Behind the plastic smile and saccharine speech often lurks gnawing hostility and festering depression.

Suffering and struggle, discouragement and doubt, death and grief are part of the human lot. Facing them squarely is an expression of faith, for honesty requires a confidence in grace which assures us that God's love is steadfast and sufficient.

Realistic hope is not wishful thinking. Faith is the willingness to live in the light of Easter, God's triumph over sin and death. It is hanging on to the promise that God is for and with us.

Our hope is rooted in God's grace-filled action in Jesus Christ, not in a form of mental gymnastics. Because God is for and with us, we can face reality with hope.

JUDGED BY OUR JUDGMENTS

THE CONVERSATION FOCUSED ON DIFFERENT TYPES OF music. The group seemed unanimous in its conclusion that Beethoven's music is "boring." Those critics judged Beethoven as an inferior musician whose music lacks appeal. Soon the conversation degenerated into an evaluation of persons who appreciate Beethoven's music. One group member judged Beethoven lovers as "stupid," "dumb," "out of it."

The encounter with these self-proclaimed music critics illustrates an important warning about passing judgment. The evaluation of Beethoven's music said more about the musical sensitivity and tastes of the critics than it said about the quality of the art they were judging. A put-down inevitably puts down the one putting down.

Whenever we pass judgment on that which transcends us we also judge ourselves. Our judgments always reveal our prejudices, priorities, values, sins, and weaknesses as much as they expose the inadequacies or quality of that which is being judged. As one person said, "People are down on what they aren't up on."

Further, judging often follows the course of the conversation about Beethoven. If Beethoven's music is inferior, then there must be something wrong with anyone who enjoys such music. In other words, if I don't like it there must be something wrong with it; and if something is wrong with it, then anyone who does appreciate it must be inferior.

Judgment easily moves from objective evaluation or humble sharing of preferences to subjective, irresponsible, and cruel rejection of persons. Such judgment becomes a form of violence, and it exposes the shallowness and egocentricity of the one passing judgment.

Maybe that is what Jesus had in mind when he warned: "'Judge not, that you be not judged. For with the judgment you pronounce you will be judged . . .'" (Matt. 7:1–2 RSV).

PRAYER IS MORE THAN CEREMONIAL

P RAYER IS ROUTINELY INCLUDED ON THE AGENDA OF MANY public events. Sports activities, civic meetings, legislative sessions, political conventions, and inauguration festivities are among the events that frequently include formal prayer. The blessing of God is invoked on activities ranging from the sublime to the ridiculous.

Raising questions about such use of prayer runs the risk of appearing to be against prayer. Of course, the courts have raised questions about the constitutionality of prayer at public school events and a few other places. My concerns are more theological than constitutional.

For one thing, a ceremonial prayer is usually controlled by the ceremony itself, not by one's relationship with God. When I was asked several years ago to deliver the invocation at a Tennessee-Kentucky football game, my directives included a twenty-five second time limit. The prayer had to fit the precise schedule in order to accommodate the TV coverage. I felt as though the prayer was reduced to no more than a twenty-five second commercial for the Almighty in the midst of "Rocky-Top" and the introduction of the football players who were cheered much longer than twenty-five seconds.

Furthermore, ceremonial prayer is usually directed toward the crowd rather than toward God. It is likely that the person praying is more aware of the presence of people than the presence of God. There follows the temptation "to be heard for their much speaking." Prayer then becomes performance or a mini-sermon.

Also, ceremonial prayer runs the risk of trivializing prayer and magnifying the trivial. Invoking the blessing of the transcendent God bestows a certain transcendent importance to the event. Prayer in such a context often invites jokes and sneers, as when the minister prayed at a University of Tennessee football game ". . . and a trip to the Peach Bowl would be nice."

Prayer, as honest communication with God, judges, inspires, transforms, renews, and guides. We must guard against permitting it to be reduced to a polite ceremonial activity that trivializes the magnificent and magnifies the trivial.

A SPRINGTIME WALK AND WORSHIP

SPRINGTIME WALKS THROUGH THE NEIGHBORHOOD IN Nashville where we live refresh and cleanse my soul. Blooming pink and white dogwoods and cotton-colored Bradford pear trees line the boulevards. Lawns trimmed with red, purple and white azaleas and sprinkled with multicolored tulips decorate the landscape. The smell of freshly mowed, springtime grass mingles with the fragrance of nature's annual floral extravaganza.

The arrival of spring has intensified my awareness of the debris along the roadway in our neighborhood. Even the smallest litter seems terribly out of place amid the resplendent beauty. I, almost subconsciously, pick up chewing gum wrappers, cigarette fragments, styrofoam cups, etc. It is as though the radiant beauty of spring exposes the smallest particles of trash. Removing the blemishes on nature's canvas seems effortless and natural.

The late Archbishop of Canterbury's definition of worship comes to mind. William Temple said that to worship is

- to quicken the conscience by the holiness of God,
- to purge the imagination by the beauty of God,
- to open the heart to the love of God,
- to devote the will to the purposes of God.

Worship is like a springtime walk. It cleanses the soul, stretches our spirit, challenges our values, and inspires commitment to the highest and best.

In the Divine Presence the debris of our lives seems gaudy and out of place. In Love's presence, hatred and bigotry become trash. Before transcendent Truth, deceit and prejudice are obvious blemishes. When authentic goodness appears, the ugliness of sin is obvious.

Worship is our greatest need! Regular exposure of our lives to the Ultimate Source of all truth, goodness, beauty, and love will transform the world into an eternal springtime of the soul.

Taking corporate worship lightly and participating in it sporadically is worse than taking a springtime walk blindfolded.

ON BEING PATRIOTIC

PATRIOTISM IS A POWERFUL THING; IT HAS INSPIRED NOBLE, unselfish, heroic acts. Countless persons have given up everything, including life itself, as a patriotic privilege and duty. Indeed, love of country is a commendable virtue and a strong motivation.

However, let us recognize that patriotism can be used for demonic and cruel purposes. History's despots have, in the name of patriotism, perpetuated grotesque evil on innocent people. Under the banner of patriotism, Hitler exterminated six million human beings. In the name of patriotism, terrorists throughout the world explode their bombs, execute their perceived enemies, and plan widespread destruction. Politicians often appeal to the patriotic impulse or motive in order to silence opposition and gain unquestioned loyalty for their policies, their wars, their exercise of power. Such abusive appeal to love of country led Samuel Johnson to refer to patriotism as "the last refuge of a scoundrel."

Patriotism is far more than flag waving or superficial slogans such as "my country, right or wrong," or "America, love it or leave it." Neither is patriotism blind support of a policy, program, or action of the party in office. Waving the flag, quoting slogans, or uncritically supporting our country's action may very well be a denial of true patriotism.

Whatever else it may mean, patriotism involves loyalty to the principles, ideals, and goals upon which our nation was founded. Those include justice, equality, and freedom for all. The attainment of those yet unreached goals requires that we refuse to support unjust, discriminatory, and oppressive action or policy.

It is possible to use patriotism as an excuse for being unpatriotic. For example, resisting efforts for racial justice is unpatriotic. However, in the name of national loyalty, such efforts have sometimes been thwarted. Patriotism has been used as a means of silencing those who have spoken out against injustice and oppression.

The most appropriate expression of true patriotism is involvement in efforts to make justice, equality, and freedom realities for all people. That sometimes involves being critical of a particular action and refusing to support that which is a denial of the cherished dreams upon which America was founded.

SPEAKING THE TRUTH IN LOVE

IN THE HEAT OF A DEBATE ON A CONTROVERSIAL ISSUE, A man shared damaging information about a leader of the opposing side. The information expressed had nothing to do with the issue at hand. Everything he said about his opponent was factual, though irrelevant. His opponent was humiliated and demeaned before the group.

After the meeting, I asked the man why he shared the information. He responded, "I believe in telling the truth. Preacher, you of all people ought to believe in that."

Is speaking the truth always a virtue? Integrity, honesty, dependability are much-needed qualities. Nevertheless, truth can be, and often is, misused. Telling the truth, like all other noble qualities, may be perverted and abused.

It is easy to needlessly wound others in the name of speaking the truth. Sharing harmful facts about others for the purpose of enhancing one's own selfish interest is a respectable form of gossip. It is a subtle form of hatred. In the political arena it is a popular diversion from the real issues. Disprove the person and you don't have to come to grips with what that person says. That is one of the oldest fallacies of logic.

The apostle Paul shared helpful advice on the matter. To the Ephesians he wrote: "But speaking the truth in love, we must grow up in every way into him who is the head, into Christ" (4:15). He added ". . . putting away falsehood, let all of us speak the truth to our neighbors, for we are members of one another" and "Put away from you all bitterness and wrath and anger and wrangling and slander . . . and be kind to one another, tenderhearted, forgiving one another, as God in Christ has forgiven you" (4:25, 31–32).

Truth without love and concern for the well-being of the community can be vindictive, malicious, and hateful. Love without truth may be mere sentimentalism and emotionalism. Truth and love belong together.

Truth is a form of power. As is true of all forms of powers, great care must be exercised in releasing it. Truth in the service of love redeems. Truth in the service of hatred and selfishness destroys.

Since we are members one of another in the body of Christ, let us speak "the truth in love" and "grow up in every way into Him who is the head, into Christ."

HE SET HIS FACE TO GO TO JERUSALEM

JESUS HAD MOVED FROM OBSCURITY TO PROMINENCE IN A matter of months. News of his miraculous healing and challenging teaching and preaching had spread throughout the region. Crowds flocked to hear him and to benefit from his powerful presence. His disciples followed with enthusiasm and devotion. The long-awaited kingdom of God was at hand.

Then fortune began to change. The crowds got smaller. Opposition developed. The disciples' zeal began to wane. Confusion ensued. Anticipation of freedom from pain and want turned to dread of rejection and suffering. The triumph of Caesar's reign seemed more evident than the dawning of God's reign.

According to Luke's Gospel, the turning point came when Jesus said to his disciples, "'The Son of Man must undergo great suffering . . .'" and when ". . . he set his face to go to Jerusalem" (Luke 9:22, 51). Why would Jesus spoil apparent success and popularity by talking of suffering and turning toward dangerous Jerusalem?

Jerusalem was the center of political, economic, and religious power. Jesus made a conscious decision to take the announcement of God's coming reign of justice, generosity, and joy to the center of earthly power. His resolute purpose and method were made clear in his struggle in the wilderness of temptation (Matt. 4:1–11). He refused to be subservient to personal popularity, political power, or manipulative piety.

The Season of Lent has arrived. We direct our attention toward the passion of Jesus and his call to turn away from the false popular gods that promise prestige, power, and painless piety. The centers of political, economic, and religious power continue to need the challenge of the coming reign of God. Persons and congregations whose lives and witness proclaim the kingdom of God risk rejection, suffering, and even execution. Going toward a new Jerusalem is dangerous business.

The good news is this: the one who "set his face to go to Jerusalem" accompanies the disciples on their Jerusalem journeys. He went to Jerusalem, was arrested, tried, and crucified. But we know that the old Jerusalem political, economic, and religious powers did not have the last word. He triumphed! The victory has been won! Let us journey into our Jerusalems with repentance and hope!

THE BEST OF ALL IS, GOD IS WITH US

IN MID-FEBRUARY 1791, THE ELDERLY JOHN WESLEY BECAME ill. By March 1, he was barely strong enough to speak. However, much to the astonishment of those present, he gathered enough strength to sing Isaac Watts' hymn, "I'll praise My Maker While I've breath." Then, as his life began to ebb away, he uttered his last sentence. It was an affirmation of faith: "The best of all is, God is with us."

It may be a morbid thought, but I wonder what my last word will be. Will it be an affirmation of faith? A word of comfort and hope? An assurance of love? Or will it be a sigh of despair or fear? An expression of regret? A word of anger, or disappointment, or hatred? I would like for it to be Wesley's affirmation: "The best of all is, God is with us."

Of course, we may not have a choice of a last word. Wesley knew his end was near and he had maintained his mental faculties. We may not be so fortunate. Any word we speak may be our last, and biological changes may cause us to speak words we do not choose. We do, however, have a choice as to our next word, and we can so live and speak that our very lives become our last word.

Looking back over the year now gone, I would like to retrieve some words spoken. Not all my actions would I like to be my legacy. Like all other years, the experiences have been a mixture of joy and sadness, victory and defeat, affirmation of faith and sighs of doubt, words of assurance and words of anger, acts of obedience and deeds of betrayal. But, "the best of all is this, God is with us."

The new year is filled with innumerable opportunities to speak and act. Unknown challenges await us. Unexpected joy and pain will likely greet us sometime in the new year. Decisions will be made. Relationships, new and old, will be strengthened or damaged by our words and actions. The church will be stronger or weaker by what we say and do. Christ will be honored or dishonored by our attitude and behavior. But, "the best of all is, God is with us."

Richard Heitzenrater writes: "Wesley had long lived in the presence of his Maker, in fear of God's judgment and yet trusting in divine justice, in awe of God's majesty and yet confident in his gracious love, in expectation of continual surprises from God's Spirit and yet hoping through it all for guidance and comfort. So that at his death, Wesley knew of what he spoke, when from a heart that had long sought peace, he uttered his final testimony of faith, 'The best of all is, God is with us.'"

May we so live that we can proclaim "the best of all is, God is with us."